高等职业教育
工学结合系列教材·汽车类

汽车专业英语
Special English for Automobile

主 编：崔 玲
副主编：孙永丽 高大威
参 编：严 超

"互联网+"教材

全书视频资源

北京理工大学出版社
BEIJING INSTITUTE OF TECHNOLOGY PRESS

内容简介

本书包含 5 个教学任务，分别是了解汽车、发动机、底盘、车身、电气设备。每个教学任务均设有学习热身、听与说、阅读、维修保养、知识拓展 5 个环节，形式活泼，结构明快；内容难度适中，涵盖了汽车的历史文化、主要系统结构和原理、新能源汽车技术、汽车使用、保养维修等方面的知识。学生通过对本书的学习，可以全面了解汽车相关的英语专业词汇及专业知识，全面提高在实际工作岗位上运用专业英语的能力。

本书充分利用新媒体技术，建立了二维码，借以链接大量的信息化教学资源。学生通过扫描二维码，就可观看视频或者赏析更丰富的拓展内容。这样编排既可增强教学的趣味性，又能使教材具备可操作性，使学生充分利用零星的时间学习，提高学习效率。本书可供高职高专院校汽车类专业使用。

版权专有　侵权必究

图书在版编目（CIP）数据

汽车专业英语 / 崔玲主编 . —北京：北京理工大学出版社，2019.2（2021.12重印）
ISBN 978-7-5682-6552-2

Ⅰ.①汽…　Ⅱ.①崔…　Ⅲ.①汽车工程－英语－高等学校－教材　Ⅳ.① U46

中国版本图书馆 CIP 数据核字 (2019) 第 002385 号

出版发行 / 北京理工大学出版社有限公司

社　　址 / 北京市海淀区中关村南大街 5 号

邮　　编 / 100081

电　　话 /（010）68914775（总编室）
　　　　　（010）82562903（教材售后服务热线）
　　　　　（010）68948351（其他图书服务热线）

网　　址 / http://www.bitpress.com.cn

经　　销 / 全国各地新华书店

印　　刷 / 三河市天利华印刷装订有限公司

开　　本 / 787 毫米 ×1092 毫米　1/16

印　　张 / 8　　　　　　　　　　　　　　　责任编辑 / 梁铜华

字　　数 / 180 千字　　　　　　　　　　　　文案编辑 / 梁铜华

版　　次 / 2019 年 2 月第 1 版　2021 年 12 月第 4 次印刷　　责任校对 / 周瑞红

定　　价 / 24.00 元　　　　　　　　　　　　责任印制 / 李　洋

图书出现印装质量问题，请拨打售后服务热线，本社负责调换

编审委员会

主　　任　王建良
副 主 任　王福忠　丁在明　张宏坤
委　　员　刘文国　李　勇　冯益增
　　　　　许子阳　张世军　崔　玲
　　　　　孙静霞

前 言
PREFACE

  本书为2015年出版的《汽车实用英语》的第2版，并更名为《汽车专业英语》。该书第1版自出版以来多次印刷，深受广大读者的欢迎与关注。通过教学实践，我们对教材内容的处理有了一些新的看法；此外，也听取了各校教师和同学对本书的宝贵意见和建议，在此基础上，我们对第1版进行了修订。

  本书除了保持第1版的基本结构与内容外，主要对内容进行了更新与整合，删减了汽车营销、保险理赔等方面的内容，最终整合为五个教学任务。每个教学任务均设有学习热身、听与说、阅读、维修保养、知识拓展5个环节，深入浅出地介绍了汽车的历史文化、主要系统结构和原理、新能源汽车技术、汽车使用、保养维修等方面的内容，并结合高职院校教学的特点、学生的实际情况，按照英语学习规律组织教学材料，循序渐进，层层提高，培养学生在实际工作岗位上运用汽车专业英语的能力。

  另外，本书充分利用新媒体技术，建立二维码，链接大量的信息化教学资源。学生通过扫描二维码，就可观看视频或者赏析更丰富的拓展内容，这样做既能增强教学的趣味性，又能使本书具有可操作性，使学生充分利用零星时间学习，提高学习效率。

  本书由山东交通职业学院车辆工程系编写，参加编写者为崔玲、严超、孙永丽。上海理工大学的高大威参与了本版的修订工作，在教材结构、教学内容、教学安排等方面提出了许多宝贵意见。另外，在编写过程中，我们参考了大量的书籍、文献和资料，在此谨向作者一并表示衷心的感谢！

  鉴于汽车技术的不断发展及编者水平所限，书中难免存在错误或不足之处，恳请广大读者予以批评指正。

编 者

2018年10月

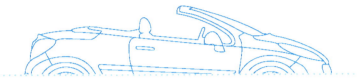

Task One
Know About Automobiles ··· 1

Part I Warming Up ··· 1
Car Logos and Car Brands ··· 1
The Development of the Car ··· 3

Part II Listening and Speaking ··· 6
Dialogue Visiting the Car Company ··· 6

Part III Reading ··· 7
Passage One BMW Logo History ··· 7
Passage Two Structure of the Automobile ··· 9

Part IV Maintenance and Repair ··· 11
Automobile Maintenance Tools ··· 11
Basic Automobile Maintenance Items ··· 12

Part V Outward Bound ··· 15
New Energy Vehicles ··· 15

Task Two
Automobile Engine ··· 21

Part I Warming Up ··· 21
Know About Automobile Engines ··· 21

Part II Listening and Speaking ··· 25
Dialogue Visiting the Engine Shop ··· 25

Part III Reading ··· 26
Passage One Construction of Internal Combustion Engines ··· 26
Passage Two How the Four-stroke Internal Combustion Engine Works ··· 31
Passage Three Hybrid Engines ··· 33

Part IV Maintenance and Repair ··· 35
How to Check the Engine Oil ··· 35

	Engine Maintenance Tips	36
Part V	Outward Bound	38
	Automobile Exhaust Gases	38

Task Three
Automobile Chassis ················· 41

Part I	Warming Up	41
	Know About the Automobile Chassis	41
Part II	Listening and Speaking	46
	Dialogue Book a Date to Repair the Car	46
Part III	Reading	46
	Passage One Main Structure of Automobile Chassis	46
	Passage Two Power Train	50
	Passage Three Power Steering System	53
	Passage Four Automobile Transmission	55
Part IV	Maintenance and Repair	57
	Auto 4S Shop	57
Part V	Outward Bound	58
	Electric Power Train	58
	Driving a Car with a CVT	60

Task Four
Automobile Body ················· 63

Part I	Warming Up	63
	Know About the Automobile Body	63
Part II	Listening and Speaking	65
	Dialogue Talking About the Crash Sensor	65
Part III	Reading	65
	Passage One Auto Body Construction	65
	Passage Two Instrument Panel	70
Part IV	Maintenance and Repair	71
	How to Remove Residue Marks Left by Other Objects	71
Part V	Outward Bound	74
	Reducing Body Weight	74

Task Five
Automobile Electrical System 77

Part I Warming Up 77
Know About Automobile Electrical System 77

Part II Listening and Speaking 82
Dialogue Automobile Introduction 82

Part III Reading 83
Passage One Automobile Electrical System 83
Passage Two Motronic Engine-management System 86
Passage Three Air Conditioning System 90
Passage Four Electronic Brakeforce Distribution 92

Part IV Maintenance and Repair 94
When to Replace Your Automobile Starter Motor 94

Part V Outward Bound 95
Electronic Stability Control 95
Maintenance Types 97

Vocabulary 99

Task One

Know About Automobiles

Task Description

(1) The development of automobiles;

(2) Automobile brands;

(3) The basic structure of the automobile.

Objectives

(1) To understand the development of automobiles, and find out the general information about the history of the automobile;

(2) To learn to talk about the structure of the automobile in English;

(3) To recognize some car logos and English names, and learn about the culture of some automobile brands.

Part I Warming Up

Car Logos and Car Brands

1. Look at the pictures of the car logos and match them with the correct names.

汽车品牌大全
中英对照

(1)

(2)

(3)

(4)

(5)　　　(6)　　　(7)　　　(8)

(9)　　　(10)　　　(11)　　　(12)

(13)　　　(14)　　　(15)　　　(16)

(17)　　　(18)　　　(19)

(20)　　　(21)　　　(22)

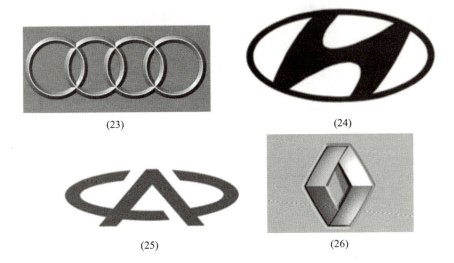

(23)   (24)

(25)   (26)

Toyota	Chrysler	Rolls-Royce	Skoda	Fiat	BMW	Volkswagen
Ferrari	Chevrolet	MAYBACH	Lexus	Ford	Audi	Lamborghini
Cadillac	Porsche	Bentley	Mazda	Buick	GM	Mercedes-Benz
Renault	Chery	EMGRAND	Hyundai	CITROEN		

2. Answer the following questions.

(1) Which brand is common in your hometown? Have you ever noticed it?

(2) Which brand would you like to choose in the future?

The Development of the Car

Look at the pictures. Discuss the differences between the four cars with your partner and complete the table.

汽车发展史

The first Benz (The first three-wheeled vehicle)

The first Daimler (The first four-wheeled automobile)

Ford Model T (The first vehicle produced by assembly line)

BMW730

汽车造型发展史

Items	The first Benz	The first Daimler	The first Ford Model T	BMW730
wheel	3 wheels: 1 small wheel in the front, 2 bigger ones in the back	4 wheels: 2 small wheels in the front	4 wheels: same size	
engine position	Behind the seat and above the axle			
seat	1			
door	none			

Vocabulary

Useful Words

logo ['ləugəu] *n.* 标识，徽标

brand [brænd] *n.* 品牌

wheel [wi:l] *n.* 车轮

engine ['endʒin] *n.* 发动机

axle ['æksəl] *n.* 车轴，轴

Proper Nouns

Toyota 丰田

Chrysler 克莱斯勒

Ferrari 法拉利

Cadillac 凯迪拉克

Porsche 保时捷

Bentley 宾利

MAYBACH 迈巴赫

Rolls-Royce 劳斯莱斯

Skoda 斯柯达

Fiat 菲亚特

BMW 宝马

Volkswagen 大众

Lamborghini 兰博基尼

Mercedes-Benz 梅赛德斯奔驰

Mazda 马自达

Buick 别克

Ford 福特

Audi 奥迪

Lexus 雷克萨斯

Chevrolet 雪佛兰

GM 通用汽车

Renault 雷诺

EMGRAND 吉利帝豪

Chery 奇瑞

Hyundai 现代

CITROEN 雪铁龙

Daimler 戴姆勒

Part Ⅱ Listening and Speaking

Dialogue   Visiting the Car Company

Receptionist (R): Welcome to our car company. I'll show you around and explain the operations as we go along.

Customer (C): That'll be most helpful.

R: This is our car company building. We have all the administrative departments here. Down there is the sales section and the advertising section.

C: How much do you spend on car advertising every year?

R: About 5% of the gross sales. Please step this way. I'd like to show you our showroom. Almost all of my company's products can be seen here.

C: Oh, what lovely cars of all kinds. If I placed an order now, how long would it be before I got delivery?

R: It would largely depend on the kind of the order you want.

C: OK. Thank you for giving me a tour of your car company.

R: My pleasure. How do you feel our car company?

C: It gave me a good picture of your cars. I would like to show your company to our friends.

R: Happy to hear that. What's your general impression on our cars, may I ask?

C: I was very impressed. I have seen some kinds of cars. Nice enough.

R: Sure. They are our latest products.

C: Thank you very much.

R: You are welcome.

Vocabulary

Useful Words

administrative [əd'ministrətiv] *adj.* 管理的，行政的
department [di'pɑ:tmənt] *n.* 部门，系，科，局
section ['sekʃən] *n.* 部门，地区，章节
gross [grəus] *adj.* 总共的
delivery [di'livəri] *n.* 交付，递送

Part Ⅲ Reading

Read the following passages and do the exercises.

Passage One BMW Logo History

According to BMW, their round blue and white logo is the movement of an aircraft propeller, showing white blades cutting through the blue sky—an explanation that BMW adopted for convenience in 1929, twelve years after the logo was created. In fact the emblem developed from the round Rapp Motorenwerke Company logo, from which the BMW company grew, combined with the white and blue colors of the flag of Bavaria to produce the BMW logo. However, the origin of the logo is in dispute. To quote an article recently posted by The New York Times: "At the BMW Museum in Munich, Anne Schmidt-possiwal explained that the blue and white company logo did not represent a spinning propeller, but was meant to show the colors of the Free State of Bavaria."

BMW logo

BMW sports car

宝马汽车的标志起源与历史

Task one 译文

Exercises

1. Answer the following questions according to the passage.

(1) What does the BMW logo represent according to BMW?

(2) Where did the BMW logo come from?

(3) What does the BMW logo really represent according to some people?

2. Translate the following paragraph in the passage into Chinese.

According to BMW, their round blue and white logo is the movement of an aircraft propeller, showing white blades cutting through the blue sky—an explanation that BMW adopted for convenience in 1929, twelve years after the logo was created.

宝马车标演变史

Vocabulary

Useful Words

aircraft ['eəkrɑːft] *n.* 飞机，航空器

propeller [prə'pelə] *n.* 螺旋桨，推进器

blade [bleid] *n.* (机器上旋转的) 叶片，桨叶；刀片

adopt [ə'dɔpt] *v.* 采取，采纳，采用

emblem ['embləm] *n.* 象征，标记

dispute [di'spjuːt] *n.* 争议，纠纷

quote [kwəut] *v.* 引用，引述

spin [spin] *v.* 使快速旋转；疾驰

Phrases and Expressions

in dispute 有争议，处于争议中

Proper Nouns

BMW (Bavarian Motor Works) 德国宝马汽车公司

Bavaria 巴伐利亚

> Rapp Motorenwerke Company 拉普发动机制造公司
>
> Munich 慕尼黑
>
> *New York Times* 《纽约时报》

Passage Two Structure of the Automobile

Thousands of individual parts make up the modern automobile. Much like the human body, these parts are arranged into several semi-independent systems, each with a different function.

An automobile is composed of four sections: the engine, chassis, body, and electrical system. The engine—the heart of the automobile—is comprised of pistons, cylinders, tubes to deliver fuel to the cylinders, and other components. Each system is necessary for making the automobile run and reducing noise and pollution.

Task one 译文

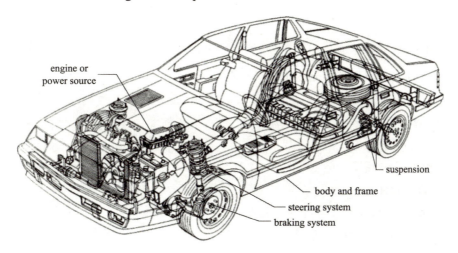

Structure of an automobile

The body of the vehicle encloses the mechanical components and passenger compartment. It is made of relatively light sheet metal or composite plastics (复合塑料). The components which make up the chassis are held together in proper relation to each other by the frame. An automobile body usually consists of a driving room, a passenger or loading room, and possibly a trunk.

The chassis includes the power train, the steering system, the braking system, the suspension system (including wheels and tires). It provides the strength necessary to support the vehicle components and the payload (有效载荷) placed upon it.

Electricity is used for many parts of the car, from the headlights to the radio, but its chief function is to provide the electrical spark needed to ignite the fuel in the cylinders.

These systems will be found in every form of motor vehicle and are designed to interact with and support each other.

Exercises

Answer the following questions according to the passage.

(1) What are the sections of an automobile?

(2) What is the most important part of an automobile?

(3) What are the functions of electricity?

Vocabulary

Useful Words

automobile ['ɔːtəməubiːl/ˌɔːtəmə'biːl] *n.* 汽车
part [pɑːt] *n.* 零部件
chassis ['ʃæsi] *n.* 底盘
body ['bɔdi] *n.* 车身
piston ['pistən] *n.* 活塞
cylinder ['silində] *n.* 气缸
component [kəm'pəunənt] *n.* 部件，元件
enclose [in'kləuz] *v.* 封闭；包装
frame [freim] *n.* 车架
trunk [trʌŋk] *n.* 行李箱
tire ['taiə] *n.* 轮胎
headlight ['hedlait] *n.* 前大灯
ignite [ig'nait] *v.* 点火，点燃

Phrases and Expressions

passenger compartment 乘客舱
electrical system 电气系统
suspension system 悬架系统
braking system 制动系统
running gear 行驶系统
drive line 传动系统

Part IV Maintenance and Repair

Automobile Maintenance Tools

1. Look at the pictures of maintenance tools and match them with their English versions.

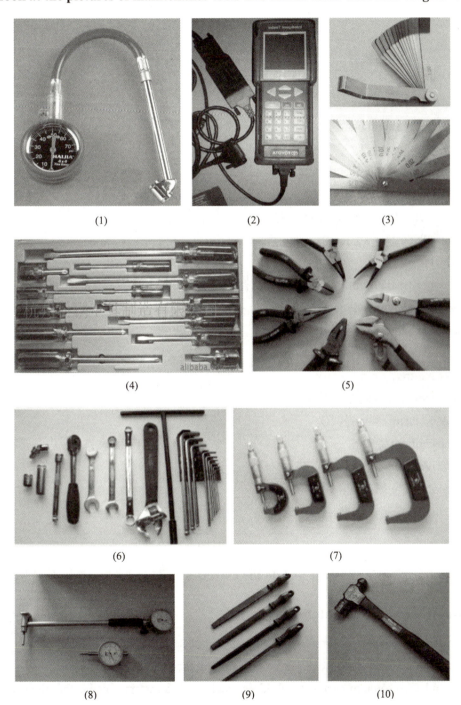

a. Hammer b. Diagnostic tester c. Pliers d. Screwdriver set e. Kinds of wrenches	f. Dial gauge g. Tire pressure gauge h. Files i. Micrometer j. Thickness gauge

Vocabulary

Useful Words

maintenance ['meintənəns] *n.* 维修，保养

gauge [geidʒ] *n.* 仪表

diagnostic [ˌdaiəg'nɔstik] *n.* 诊断

plier ['plaiə] *n.* 钳子，尖嘴钳

screwdriver ['skruːˌdraivə] *n.* 螺丝刀

hammer ['hæmə] *n.* 锤子

file [fail] *n.* 锉刀

micrometer [mai'krɔmitə] *n.* 千分尺，测微计

Phrases and Expressions

auto maintenance 汽车保养

kinds of wrenches 各种扳手

Proper Nouns

tire pressure gauge 轮胎压力表

diagnostic tester 诊断测试仪

long nose pliers 尖嘴钳

screwdriver set 一套螺丝刀

thickness gauge 厚薄规，测厚仪

dial gauge 百分表

2. Read the following passage and do the exercises.

Basic Automobile Maintenance Items

Many people consider automobile maintenance a necessary evil. There are several things you can do to improve your car's performance and to protect your investment and save some money. Like children, each car has different needs that the owner should consider. Automobile maintenance should be a top priority for any car owner.

Task one 译文

Auto maintenance items

Here are some basic maintenance items and intervals.

- Engine oil: every 3,000 miles or 3 months, unless you use Mobil One, in which case 6,000 miles or 6 months.
- Fuel filter: 35,000 - 40,000 miles.
- Air filter and AC air filter: as needed.
- Spark plugs: conventional plugs, 30,000 miles; double platinum, 50,000 miles.
- Coolant flush: 2 years/24,000 miles.
- Brake fluid flush and power steering fluid flush: 2 years or when dirty or discolored.
- Fuel injection system service: 40,000 miles.
- Tire rotation: 5,000 - 8,000 miles.
- Wheel alignment: 15,000 - 20,000 miles.

汽车保养小常识

Exercises

1. Answer the following questions according to the passage.

(1) Why should automobile maintenance be a top priority for any car owner?

(2) What maintenance items are mentioned in the passage?

(3) Can you name some other maintenance items?

2. Match the following expressions with their Chinese versions.

(1) automobile performance	a. 燃油滤清器
(2) maintenance interval	b. 制动液
(3) fuel filter	c. 汽车性能
(4) brake fluid	d. 轮胎换位
(5) tire rotation	e. 车轮定位
(6) wheel alignment	f. 保养周期

Vocabulary

Useful Words

priority [prai'ɔrəti] *n.* 优先考虑的事
interval ['intəvəl] *n.* 间隔；间歇
platinum ['plætinəm] *n.* 铂，白金
flush [flʌʃ] *v.* 冲洗，清洗
discolored [dis'kʌlərd] *adj.* 变色的，脱色的
throttle ['θrɔtl] *n.* 节气门，油门
rotation [rəu'teiʃən] *n.* 旋转，转动

Phrases and Expressions

power steering 动力转向，转向助力装置
fuel injection system 燃油喷射系统
throttle body 节气门体
automobile performance 汽车性能
maintenance interval 保养周期
fuel filter 燃油滤清器
brake fluid 制动液
tire rotation 轮胎换位
wheel alignment 车轮定位

Proper Nouns

Mobil One 美孚 1 号
AC 空调 air conditioner 的缩写

Part V Outward Bound

Read the following passage and do the exercises.

New Energy Vehicles

New energy vehicles are the vehicles which use non-conventional motor vehicle fuels as a power source (or use conventional fuel, but adopt a new vehicle power unit), integrated advanced vehicle control and drive technology, with advanced technical principles, new technologies, and new structures. They are good for the environment, saving gas, reducing CO_2 emissions, and using recycled materials.

Task one 译文

New energy vehicles include hybrid vehicles, pure electric vehicles (including solar cars), fuel cell electric vehicles, hydrogen vehicles, and other new energy vehicles.

A hybrid car depends on two kinds of engines for propulsion power. Most hybrid cars available today use a combination of gasoline and electric engines while some use a combination of diesel and electric engines. A hybrid car combines the strengths of each type of engines. It produces less pollution and it is more economical than the conventional car, while still being more powerful than electric cars.

Hybrid electrical vehicle—Lexus LS600hL

了解新能源汽车发展史

混合动力超级汽车的未来

Electric car—Nissan NUVU

An electric car is a plug-in battery powered automobile which is propelled by electric motor(s). Electric cars have the potential to reduce city pollution through having zero emissions. For shorter journeys, electric cars are practical forms of transportation and can be inexpensively recharged overnight.

Solar car

A hydrogen car runs mainly on either a hydrogen fuel source like that of an internal combustion engine, or on a fuel cell like that of an electric car. The hydrogen car could be the future of cars, as alternative energies are being explored more and more, and hydrogen technology is becoming increasingly practical.

Hydrogen vehicle

GM Sequel (a hydrogen fuel cell car)

 A fuel cell powered car looks just like other cars on the road today, but they're cleaner, quieter, more efficient, and work very differently. When you turn the key, hydrogen and compressed air flow to the fuel cell module. A fuel cell engine consists of a proton exchange membrane fuel cell module, coupled with the systems required in a typical automotive engine. The electricity produced by the fuel cell is delivered to the electric drive system in the vehicle, which changes electric power into mechanical energy and drives the wheels of the car.

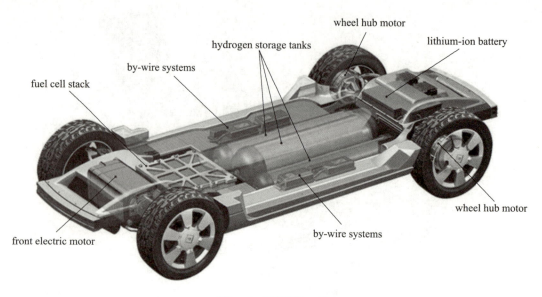

Chassis of GM Sequel

Exercises

1. Decide whether the following statements are true (T) or false (F) according to the passage.

(1) New energy vehicles use conventional fuel as a power source. (   )

(2) New energy vehicles are both fuel-efficient and environmentally-friendly. (   )

(3) Hybrid cars either use a combination of a gasoline and electric engines or diesel and electric engines. (   )

(4) Electric cars have the advantage of zero emissions and can be expensively recharged overnight. (   )

(5) The hydrogen car will definitely replace the modern car as hydrogen technology becomes increasingly practical. (   )

2. Choose the best answer to each question.

(1) Which of the following is not an advantage of fuel cell powered cars?

A. Cleaner.   B. More efficient.

C. Faster.   D. Quieter.

(2) The electricity used in the car is produced by _____.

A. a generator   B. a fuel cell

C. an engine   D. a battery

3. Translate the following sentences into Chinese.

(1) They are good for the environment, saving gas, reducing CO_2 emissions, and using recycled materials.

(2) A hybrid car depends on two kinds of engines for propulsion power.

(3) An electric car is a plug-in battery powered automobile which is propelled by electric motor(s).

(4) A hydrogen car runs mainly on either a hydrogen fuel source like that of an internal combustion engine, or on a fuel cell like that of an electric car.

Vocabulary

Useful Words

integrate ['intigreit] *v.* 使一体化，使合并
principle ['prinsəpl] *n.* 工作原理
emission [i'miʃən] *n.* 排放，排放物，散发物
recycle [ˌriː'saikl] *v.* 回收利用，再利用
propulsion [prəu'pʌlʃən] *n.* 推进，推进力
combination [ˌkɔmbi'neiʃn] *n.* 结合，联合
potential [pə'tenʃəl] *n.* 潜力，潜能
inexpensively [ˌinik'spensivli] *adv.* 廉价地，便宜地
recharge [riː'tʃɑːdʒ] *v.* 再充电
overnight [ˌəuvə'nait] *adv.* 一夜间，通宵
proton ['prəutɔn] *n.* 质子
membrane ['membrein] *n.* 膜，薄膜

Phrases and Expressions

plug-in battery 插入式电池
fuel cell module 燃料电池组
couple with 与……相结合，伴随

Task Two

Automobile Engine

(1) The function and types of automobile engines;
(2) The basic structure of the internal combustion engine;
(3) How the four-stroke internal combustion engine works;
(4) A hybrid engine.

(1) To know about the importance and the types of the automobile engine;
(2) To learn the basic structure and principle of the internal combustion engine;
(3) To learn how a hybrid engine works.

Part I   Warming Up

Know About Automobile Engines

1. Work with your partner and answer the following questions.

(1) What is the automobile engine?

(2) What is the function of the automobile engine? Why is it important to the automobile?

(3) Talk about the different types of automobile engines you know.

(4) What are the two mechanisms and five systems?

(5) Talk about the main components of the two mechanisms and five systems you know.

2. Look at the following pictures, and know about the different types of engines.

BMW 6-cylinder gasoline engine

Benz 6-cylinder gasoline engine

JAGUAR diesel engine

Four-stroke engine

Two-stroke engine

A cylinder from an air-cooled engine

A single-cylinder motorcycle engine

A multi-cylinder engine

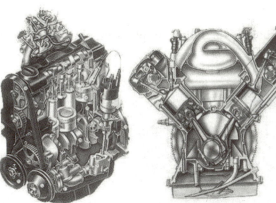
Inline   V-type

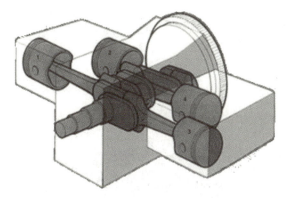
Horizontally opposed

Vocabulary

Useful Words

stroke [strəuk] *n.* 冲程，行程

horizontally [ˌhɔri'zɔntli] *adv.* 水平地

oppose [ə'pəuz] *v.* 使相对，对立

Phrases and Expressions

gasoline engine 汽油机

diesel engine 柴油机

four-stroke engine 四冲程发动机

air-cooled engine 风冷发动机

multi-cylinder engine 多缸发动机

single-cylinder engine 单缸发动机

3. Look at the following pictures, and know about the two mechanisms and five systems of engines.

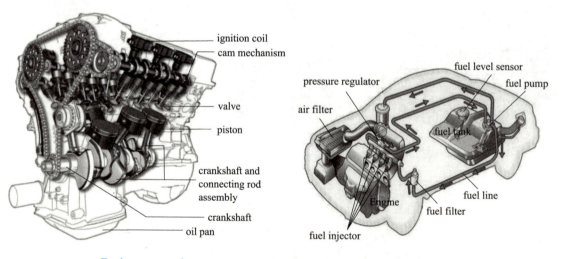

Engine construction

Fuel system

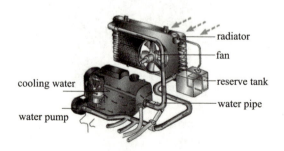

Cooling system

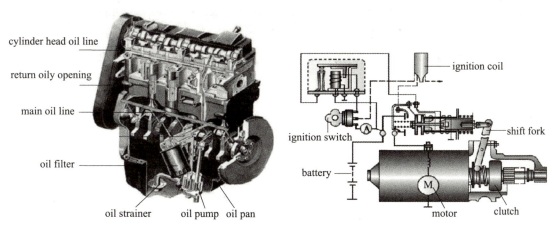

Lubricating system   Starting system

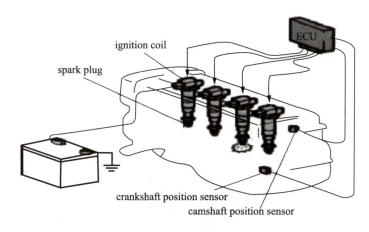

Ignition system

Part II Listening and Speaking

Dialogue Visiting the Engine Shop

A: Welcome to our company, Mr. John. Here is our engine shop.

B: Fine. Would you like to explain the details about your engines?

A: OK. This is our latest development. We put it on the market just one week ago.

B: Oh, it looks so greatly. How long was the engine developed by you?

A: For five years. Have you come up with any ideas about our latest engines?

B: Yes. As a matter of fact, I have a few ideas to tell you.

A: OK, Mr. John, please.

B: I think you should have a news conference for your new engines.

A: You are right, Mr. John.

Task two 译文

B: As I know, there are still many people who are strangers to your latest engines.

A: What next step shall we take?

B: You can introduce your new products and invite your customers to visit the engine shop.

A: Very well. That's a good idea.

Vocabulary

Phrases and Expressions

news conference 记者招待会，新闻发布会

Part Ⅲ　Reading

Task two 译文

Read the following passages and do the exercises.

Passage One　Construction of Internal Combustion Engines

There are various types of engines such as electric motors, steam engines, internal combustion engines and hybrid engines. But, the internal combustion engine is the most commonly used in the automotive field. The internal combustion engine means that the engine burns fuel within the cylinders, and converts the heat energy of fuel combustion into mechanical force used to propel the vehicle. According to the different fuels used, internal combustion engines are commonly divided into gasoline engines and diesel engines.

汽车引擎的工作原理

Engine (one camshaft)

The engine which is called the "heart" of a vehicle is used to supply power for an automobile. It includes two mechanisms and five systems. The two mechanisms are crankshaft and connecting rod assembly, valve and valve train. The five systems are fuel system, lubricating system, cooling system, ignition system and starting system.

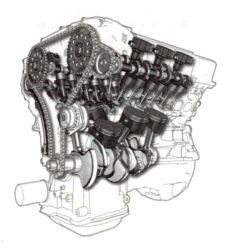

Engine (double camshafts)

发动机结构

The engine block forms the main framework, or foundation, of the engine.

The cylinders are circular, tube-like openings in the block, which act as guides for the pistons as they move up and down.

The water jackets are open spaces between the inner and outer surfaces of the block and cylinders through which the coolant flows.

The piston is a movable part that receives the pressure from the burning air/fuel mixture and converts this pressure into reciprocating motion.

Piston clearance is the distance between the outer circumference of the piston and the cylinder wall itself.

There are two types of piston rings, compression and oil control. The compression rings, which fit into the upper rig grooves, primarily seal against the loss of air/fuel mixture as the piston compresses it and also the combustion pressure as the mixture burns.

The oil control rings usually fit into the lower ring grooves. Their function is to prevent excessive amounts of oil from working up into the combustion chamber.

The crankshaft is the main rotating member, or shaft, of the engine.

The function of the crankshaft:

(1) To change the reciprocating motion of the piston to rotary along with the connecting rod.

(2) To drive the camshaft through timing gears or a timing chain and sprockets.

(3) To operate the accessories via a system of belts and pulleys.

The flywheel, a heavy wheel, is attached to the end of the crankshaft. Its function is to help the engine run smoothly by absorbing some of the energy during power stroke and release it during the other strokes.

发动机组装

汽车发动机工作原理
3D 模拟仿真动画

The basic components of the internal combustion engine are the following pictures.

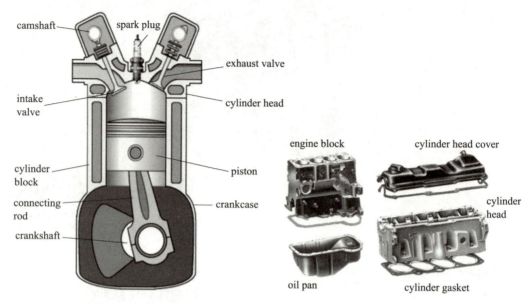

Engine components (1)

Engine components (2)

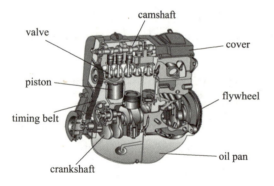

Engine components (3)

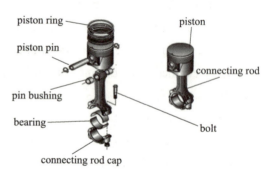

Piston and connecting rod set

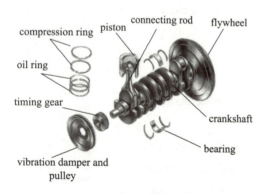

Crankshaft and connecting rod assembly

Valve and valve train

Lubricating system

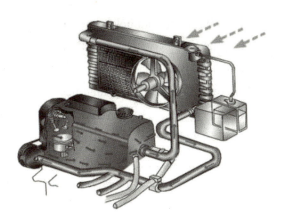

Cooling system

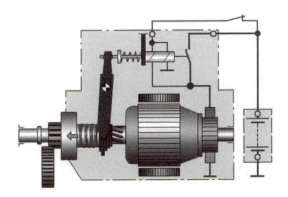

Starting system

Exercises

1. Answer the following questions according to the passage.

(1) What is the purpose of the connecting rod?

(2) What is the main framework of an engine?

(3) What are the two types of piston rings?

(4) What is the function of the flywheel?

2. Fill in the blanks below, and translate the sentences into Chinese.

(1) The _____ which is called the "heart" of a vehicle is used to supply _____ for an automobile.

(2) Power is produced by the linear motion of a piston in a _____.

(3) The _____ engine means the engine burns the fuel within the cylinders.

(4) It is well-known that the automobile is composed of four sections such as _____, _____, _____, _____.

(5) In the internal combustion engine, an air/fuel mixture is introduced into a closed _____ where it is compressed and then ignited.

Vocabulary

Useful Words

propel [prəu'pel] *v.* 推进，驱动

coolant ['ku:lənt] *n.* 冷却液

crankshaft ['kræŋkʃɑ:ft] *n.* 曲轴

camshaft ['kæmʃɑ:ft] *n.* 凸轮轴

circumference [sə'kʌmfərəns] *n.* 圆周，周长

accessory [ək'sesəri] *n.* 附件

pulley ['puli] *n.* 皮带轮，滑轮

flywheel ['flaiwi:l] *n.* 飞轮

Phrases and Expressions

internal combustion engine 内燃机

hybrid engine 混合动力发动机

fuel system 燃料系统

lubricating system 润滑系统

cooling system 冷却系统

ignition system 点火系统

starting system 起动系统

engine block 缸体

water jacket 水套

air/fuel mixture 可燃混合气

convert...into 把……转化成

piston clearance 活塞间隙

reciprocating motion 往复运动

cylinder wall 气缸壁

timing gear 正时齿轮

compression ring 气环

oil control ring 油环

combustion chamber 燃烧室

connecting rod 连杆

timing chain and sprockets 正时链条和链轮

Passage Two How the Four-stroke Internal Combustion Engine Works

Conventional cars use what is called a four-stroke combustion cycle to convert gasoline into motion. The four strokes are intake stroke, compression stroke, power stroke, and exhaust stroke. Since the same process occurs in each cylinder, we will take a look at one cylinder to see how the four-cycle process works.

Task two 译文

　　Intake　　　Compression　　　Power　　　Exhaust

四冲程发动机的工作原理

1. Intake Stroke

As the piston starts down on the intake stroke, the intake valve opens and the air/fuel mixture is drawn into the cylinder. When the piston reaches the bottom of the intake stroke, the intake valve closes, trapping the air/fuel mixture in the cylinder.

2. Compression Stroke

After the piston reaches the bottom dead center (BDC), it moves upward again and compresses the trapped air/fuel mixture that was brought in by the intake stroke. The amount that the mixture is compressed is determined by the compression ratio of the engine. As the piston reaches the top dead center (TDC) during its upward travel, the compression stroke of the piston is over.

3. Power Stroke

Before the piston reaches the TDC on the compression stroke, the spark plug fires, igniting the compressed air/fuel mixture which produces a powerful expansion of the vapor. The combustion process pushes the piston down the cylinder with great force, turning the crankshaft to provide the power to propel the vehicle. Each piston fires at a different time, determined by the engine firing order. By the time the crankshaft completes two revolutions, each cylinder in the engine will have gone through one power stroke.

发动机工作原理

4. Exhaust Stroke

Near the end of the downward movement of the piston on the power stroke, the exhaust valve opens to allow the burned exhaust gas to be expelled to the exhaust system. Since the cylinder contains so much pressure, when the valve opens, the gas is expelled with a violent force (That is why a vehicle without a muffler sounds so loud). The piston travels up to the top of the cylinder, pushing all the exhaust out before closing the exhaust valve in preparation for starting the four-stroke process over again.

Exercises

1. Translate the following expressions into English.

(1) 压缩比

(2) 进气行程

(3) 发动机点火顺序

(4) 排气消音器

(5) 可燃混合气

(6) 废气

(7) 压缩行程

(8) 做功行程

(9) 排气行程

(10) 四冲程循环内燃机

2. Select the proper word or phrase to complete each of the sentences correctly.

(1) The four-stroke cycle operates in the following order: _____.

  A. intake, compression, power, and exhaust

  B. compression, power, intake, and exhaust

  C. intake, exhaust, power, and compression

  D. intake, power, exhaust, and compression

(2) The combustion process pushes the piston down the cylinder with great force, turning the crankshaft to provide the power to _____ the vehicle.

    A. expel   B. enforce   C. propel   D. add

(3) With the _____ at the bottom of the cylinder, the exhaust valve opens to allow the burned exhaust gas to be expelled to the exhaust system.

    A. piston   B. valve   C. camshaft   D. crankshaft

(4) Each piston fires at a different time, determined by _____.

    A. the intake stroke   B. the engine firing order

    C. the compression ratio   D. the exhaust gas

3. Fill in the blanks below, and translate the following sentences into Chinese.

(1) The four piston strokes are _____, _____, _____, and _____.

(2) The engine cycle has only one _____ where the piston is actually driving the crankshaft.

(3) The intake stroke of a four-cycle engine begins with the piston at _____.

Vocabulary

Useful Words

trap [træp] *v.* 诱捕

exhaust [ig'zɔːst] *v.* 排气，排出

muffler ['mʌflə] *n.* 消音器

revolution [ˌrevə'ljuːʃən] *n.* 转，圈，旋转，循环

Phrases and Expressions

intake stroke 进气行程

compression stroke 压缩行程

power stroke 做功行程

exhaust stroke 排气行程

intake valve 进气门

bottom dead center (BDC) 下止点

compression ratio 压缩比

top dead center (TDC) 上止点

firing order 点火顺序

go through 经历，参加

exhaust valve 排气门

Passage Three   Hybrid Engines

Hybrid engines are described as the engines that combine two or more sources of power, generally gasoline and electricity. There are two types of gasoline-electric hybrid: the parallel hybrid, and the series hybrid. Both use gasoline-electric hybrid technology, but in radically different ways.

Task two 译文

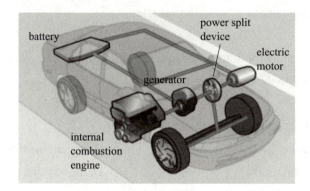

Hybrid system

本田混合动力电动汽车系统演示

In a parallel hybrid system, a gasoline engine and an electric motor work together to move the car forward, while in a series hybrid system, the gasoline engine either directly powers an electric motor that powers the vehicle, or charges batteries that will power the motor. Both types of hybrids use a process called regenerative braking to store the kinetic energy generated by the brake in the batteries, which will in turn power the electric motor.

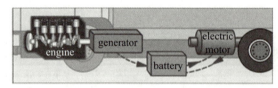

Series hybrid

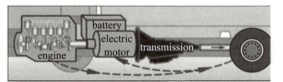

Parallel hybrid

Both parallel and series hybrid cars have small gasoline engines and produce much less pollution than standard gasoline cars, but also produce much less power. To overcome this power gap, hybrid cars are constructed with ultra lightweight materials like carbon fiber or aluminum.

Exercises

1. Match the English phrases from the passage with their Chinese meanings.

(　　) (1) parallel hybrid　　　　　　a. 动能

(　　) (2) series hybrid　　　　　　　b. 碳纤维

(　　) (3) regenerative braking　　　　c. 节油效率

(　　) (4) kinetic energy　　　　　　 d. 并联式混合动力

(　　) (5) carbon fiber　　　　　　　e. 再生制动 (回馈制动)

(　　) (6) fuel economy　　　　　　　f. 串联式混合动力

2. Fill in the table according to the passage.

Items	Differences	Similarities
The parallel hybrid		
The series hybrid		

Vocabulary

Useful Words

radically ['rædikəli] *adv.* 彻底地，根本地
brake [breik] *n.* 制动器；制动
battery ['bætəri] *n.* 蓄电池，电池
gap [gæp] *n.* 间隙，空白，缺口
aluminum [ə'ljuːminəm] *n.* 铝
generator ['dʒenəreitə] *n.* 发电机，发生器

Phrases and Expressions

hybrid engine 混合动力发动机
parallel hybrid 并联式混合动力
series hybrid 串联式混合动力
electric motor 电动机
regenerative braking 再生制动，反馈制动
kinetic energy 动能
carbon fiber 碳纤维

Part Ⅳ　Maintenance and Repair

How to Check the Engine Oil

Engine oil has limited life—after a certain point it starts losing lubricating qualities and carbonizing. Once it happens, the engine gets contaminated with carbon deposits (sludge) that significantly shorten the engine's life.

Then, how to check the engine oil?

Place your car at the level spot. Stop the engine. Wait for a while to let the engine oil pour down to the oil pan. Pull out the engine oil dipstick, and wipe it off with a clean rag or tissue. Then put it back all the way down into its place. Now, pull the dipstick again and check the oil level. Normally it should be be-

Task two 译文

更换机油、机油滤清器

tween the "FULL" and "LOW" marks. Check the oil condition: if it's too black, it's definitely time to change it. If it's slightly brown, it's OK. If it's dark brown, but still transparent, it's acceptable but it's better to change it soon.

Checking the engine oil

Engine Maintenance Tips

It is important to keep the engine in good shape. The following are some tips for doing that.

Engine compartment

(1) Regular oil change is the most important factor in keeping the engine running. If you do it more often than suggested by the manufacturer's schedule, that's even better.

(2) Always preheat the engine before starting it—especially during break-in.

(3) Try to avoid engine overheating.

(4) Changing spark plugs, air filter, timing belt, and other items based on the maintenance schedule will save you from expensive repairs.

(5) Fix any small problem right away before it causes a serious damage.

Exercises

Choose the best answers to the following questions according to the passage.

(1) How many tips are there on maintaining the engine?

    A. 3.   B. 4.

    C. 5.   D. 6.

(2) What should you do before you start the engine?

    A. Preheat the engine.   B. Put the engine up.

    C. Change the spark plugs.   D. Change the oil.

(3) Which of the following is NOT a good idea?

    A. Don't store the engine with fuel in the tank.

    B. Avoid engine overheating.

    C. Change the timing belt based on the maintenance schedule.

    D. Change the air filter as often as possible.

Vocabulary

Useful Words

oil [ɔil] *n.* 油，石油，机油

carbonize ['kɑːbənaiz] *v.* 碳化

contaminate [kən'tæmiˌneit] *v.* 污染，弄脏

deposit [di'pɔzit] *n.* 深沉物，沉积物

dipstick ['dipstik] *n.* 量油尺，测深尺

tissue ['tisjuː] *n.* 纸巾

rag [ræg] *n.* 抹布，碎布

transparent [træn'spærənt] *adj.* 透明的，清澈的

manufacturer [ˌmænju'fæktʃərə] *n.* 制造商；生产厂商

schedule ['ʃədjuːəl/'skedʒuːəl] *n.* 计划表；一览表；时间表

overheating [ˌəuvər'hiːtiŋ] *n.* 发动机过热

preheat [priː'hiːt] *v.* 预热

Phrases and Expressions

pour down 往下流

oil pan 油盘，油底壳

wipe off 擦去，抹去

all the way 一直，从头到尾，完全地

in good shape 处于良好状态

> break-in 磨合；试用
> fuel tank 油箱
> spark plug 火花塞
> air filter 空气滤清器
> timing belt 正时皮带

Part V Outward Bound

Automobile Exhaust Gases

The exhaust emissions of automotive engines contain a number of harmful pollutants. In order to minimize the amount of harmful pollutants being produced, manufacturers have developed automotive emission controls. The following is a list of the harmful exhaust gases manufacturers plan to reduce, which includes how the gases are formed and why they are dangerous.

Task two 译文

Automobile exhaust gases

1. Carbon Monoxide (CO)

Carbon Monoxide consists of carbon and oxygen. This colorless, odorless, poisonous gas is the product of incomplete combustion. By weight, carbon monoxide accounts for the 47% of air pollution.

2. Hydrocarbon (CH)

Hydrocarbon consists of carbon and hydrogen. Hydrocarbon is emitted in an unburned form from the equipment which uses a petroleum product as a source of fuel. Hydrocarbon is one of the key elements responsible for the production of photochemical smog.

3. Oxides of Nitrogen (NO_x)

Oxides of nitrogen consist of nitrogen combined with varying amounts of oxygen. NO_x are produced by heat and pressure during the combustion process. NO_x are also a main component in smog.

4. Photochemical Smog

Photochemical smog, commonly referred to simply as smog, is a by-product of the combination of HC and NO_x. In the presence of sunlight these two elements form ozone (O_3), nitrogen dioxide, and nitrogen nitrate, all of which cause respiratory problems. Nitrogen dioxide is a light brown colored gas which can affect visibility in the air corridors around major airport terminals and above highways.

5. Particulates

Particulates are tiny particles of liquids and solids which are dispersed into the atmosphere during any burning process. Particulates are composed of carbon, ash, oil, grease, and metal oxides. Smoke, haze, and dust are types of air pollution which are readily visible and are known to complicate respiratory problems caused by smog.

6. Sulfur Oxides (SO_x)

Sulfur oxides consist of various amounts of oxygen and sulfur. Sulfur oxides result from the burning of lower grades of fossil fuels, such as coal or oil.

Vocabulary

Useful Words

monoxide [mə'nɔkˌsaid] *n.* 一氧化物

oxygen ['ɔksidʒən] *n.* 氧，氧气

odorless ['əudəlis] *adj.* 没有气味的，无臭的

poisonous ['pɔizənəs] *adj.* 有毒的；有害的；恶意的

hydrocarbon [ˌhaidrə'kɑ:bən] *n.* [化] 碳氢化合物，烃

petroleum [pi'trəuliəm] *n.* 石油

ozone ['əuzəun] *n.* [化] 臭氧；清新空气

respiratory ['respərətəri] *adj.* 呼吸的

particulate [pə'tikjəlit] *n.* 微粒，粒子

atmosphere ['ætməsfiə] *n.* 大气，空气

ash [æʃ] *n.* 灰，灰烬

grease [gri:s] *n.* 动物油脂

haze [heiz] *n.* 烟雾；迷蒙

sulfur ['sʌlfə] *n.* 硫黄，硫

Phrases and Expressions

photochemical smog 光化学烟雾

oxide of nitrogen 氮氧化合物

nitrogen dioxide 二氧化氮
nitrogen nitrate 氮—硝酸盐
airport terminal 机场航道
fossil fuel 化石燃料

Task Three

Automobile Chassis

(1) The main structure of automobile chassis;
(2) The basic function of the four systems of automobile chassis;
(3) The components of the power train.

(1) To know about the importance of the automobile chassis;
(2) To learn the main parts of the automobile chassis;
(3) To learn the function of the braking system, power train, steering system, and suspension system.

Part I Warming Up

Know About the Automobile Chassis

1. Work with your partner and answer the following questions.

(1) How many systems does the automobile chassis include? What are they?

(2) Talk about the main components of the automobile chassis you know.

(3) Talk about the main components of the power train you know.

(4) What is the function of the brake system? Talk about the main components of the brake system.

Auto chassis

2. Look at the following pictures, and can you tell about the correct English names and their Chinese versions of these components?

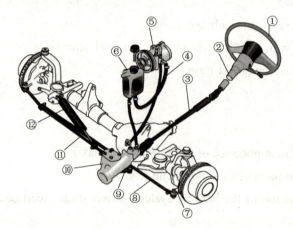

Steering system

①方向盘 _____　　②转向管柱 _____　　③转向轴 _____

④软管 _____　　⑤液压泵 _____　　⑥储液罐 _____

⑦转向节臂 _____　　⑧转向横拉杆 _____　　⑨转向摇臂 _____

⑩一体式动力转向器 _____　　⑪转向横拉杆 _____

⑫转向减振器 _____

A. steering wheel

B. steering column

C. steering shaft

D. hose

E. hydraulic pump

F. fluid reservoir

G. steering arm

H. tie rod

I. pitman arm

J. integral power steering gear

K. tie rod

L. steering damper

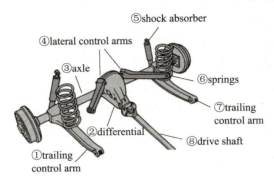

Suspension system

① _____ ② _____ ③ _____ ④ _____
⑤ _____ ⑥ _____ ⑦ _____ ⑧ _____

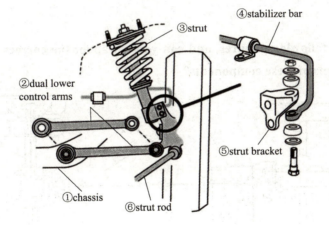

Suspension system

① _____ ② _____ ③ _____ ④ _____
⑤ _____ ⑥ _____

Vocabulary

Useful Words

strut [strʌt] *n.* 支柱，支撑杆

hose [həuz] *n.* 软管

spring [spriŋ] *n.* 弹簧

differential [ˌdifə'renʃəl] *n.* 差速器

Phrases and Expressions

stabilizer bar 横向稳定杆

steering wheel 方向盘

steering column 转向管柱

steering shaft 转向轴

hydraulic pump 液压泵

fluid reservoir 储液罐

steering arm 转向节臂

pitman arm 转向摇臂

integral power steering gear 一体式动力转向器

tie rod 转向横拉杆

steering damper 转向减振器

shock absorber 减振器

3. Look at the following pictures, and can you tell about the correct English names and their Chinese versions of these components?

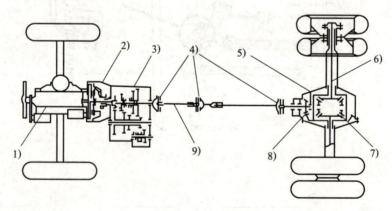

Drive line sketch map

1) 发动机 _____   2) 离合器 _____   3) 变速器 _____
4) 万向节 _____   5) 驱动桥 _____   6) 半轴 _____
7) 差速器 _____   8) 主减速器 _____   9) 传动轴 _____

1) engine   2) universal joint   3) differential   4) clutch   5) drive axle
6) final drive   7) transmission   8) wheel axle   9) drive shaft

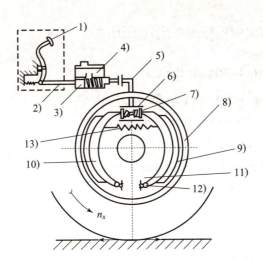

Braking system sketch map

1) 制动踏板 _____ 2) 推杆 _____ 3) 主缸活塞 _____
4) 制动主缸 _____ 5) 油管 _____ 6) 制动轮缸 _____
7) 轮缸活塞 _____ 8) 制动鼓 _____ 9) 摩擦片 _____
10) 制动蹄 _____ 11) 制动底板 _____ 12) 支撑销 _____
13) 回位弹簧 _____

1) brake pedal   2) push rod   3) master cylinder piston
4) master cylinder   5) pipeline   6) wheel cylinder
7) wheel cylinder piston   8) drum brake   9) friction plate
10) brake shoe   11) brake base plate   12) hold pin
13) retainer spring

Vocabulary

Phrases and Expressions

brake pedal 制动踏板
push rod 推杆
master cylinder 制动主缸
wheel cylinder 制动轮缸
master cylinder piston 主缸活塞
wheel cylinder piston 轮缸活塞
friction plate 摩擦片
brake base plate 制动底板
retainer spring (制动蹄) 回位弹簧

Part II Listening and Speaking

Dialogue Book a Date to Repair the Car

A: Hello, Benz 4S Shop. What can I do for you?

B: Hello, I'd like to book a date to repair my car.

A: What's wrong with your car?

B: The wheels seem to pull to one side when I drive it.

A: Have you checked the tire inflation?

B: Yes. It's all right.

A: What about the tire wear?

B: There's no problem, either.

A: Oh. Is the day after tomorrow convenient for you?

B: Yes. That is OK.

A: Fine. Please come here on July 15th. Mr. Yu will help you with the car.

B: Thank you.

A: My pleasure.

Vocabulary

Useful Words

inflation [in'fleiʃən] *n.* 膨胀，充气

wear [weə] *n.* 磨损

Part III Reading

Read the following passages and do the exercises.

Passage One Main Structure of Automobile Chassis

The four main systems of automobile chassis are the power train (or drive line), the steering system, the suspension system and the braking system. (The power train is introduced in the next passage.)

Automobile chassis

1. **Steering System**

The steering system is the means by which the driver of a vehicle is able to control the position of the front wheels. The system must provide ease of handling, good directional control, and stability. This is achieved by the steering system in conjunction with the suspension system.

观致汽车底盘
结构测评视频

Steering system (1)

There are two types of steering systems, namely the manual steering system and power steering system. The power steering system includes the hydraulic power steering system, electric power steering (EPS) and electric hydraulic power steering system (EHPS). The key components that make up the steering system are the steering wheel, steering column, steering shaft, steering gear, pitman arm, drag link, steering arm, ball joints, and tie-rod assembly. The hydraulic power steering system adds a hydraulic pump, fluid reservoir, hoses, and either a power assist unit mounted on, or integral with a steering gear assembly.

Steering system (2)

2. **Suspension System**

The suspension system has the following functions:
To keep a car's wheels in firm contact with the road.
To provide a comfortable ride for the passengers.

哈弗汽车底盘

To provide steering stability with good handling.

There are three fundamental components of any suspension: the springs, shock absorbers and anti-sway bars (connecting linkages). Without these parts, the comfort and ease of driving would be reduced.

Suspension system

3. Braking System

底盘的认识

Automobile brakes must be able to stop the car, prevent excess speed when coasting, and hold the vehicle in position when stopped on grades. Each vehicle must have two independent brake systems for safety. The main brake system is the service brake system. The secondary is the parking brake system. The automobile brake systems are divided into three types of service brake combinations: drum brakes, disc brakes, and disc-drum combinations.

Braking system

Brake (1)

Brake (2)

Exercises

1. Answer the following questions according to the passage.

(1) What are the fundamental components that make up the suspension system?

(2) What are the classifications of steering systems?

2. Fill in the blanks below, and translate the following sentences into Chinese.

(1) Each vehicle must have two independent brake systems for safety. The main brake system is _____, and the secondary is _____.

(2) The brake system is one of the most important safety systems on the _____.

(3) The steering system is the means by which the driver of a vehicle is able to control the position of the _____.

3. Make the best answers to the following sentences.

(1) Hydraulic brake systems utilize _____ to transfer force from the driver's foot to the brake shoes.

  A. air   B. solid   C. liquid   D. linkage

(2) Automobile _____ must be able to stop the car, prevent excess speed when coasting, and hold the vehicle in position when stopped on grades.

  A. brakes   B. engine   C. transmission   D. clutch

(3) The _____ is a device for converting the rotary motion of the steering wheel into straight-line motion of linkage.

  A. engine   B. steering gear   C. transmission   D. clutch

Vocabulary

Useful Words

stability [stə'biliti] *n.* 稳定性
handle ['hændl] *v.* 操作，处理
brake [breik] *n.* 制动器
coast ['kəust] *v.* 滑行

Phrases and Expressions

power train 传动系统
drive line 传动系统
steering system 转向系统
braking system 制动系统
suspension system 悬架系统
in conjunction with 连同，共同，与……协力
anti-sway bar 稳定杆
manual steering system 手动转向系统，机械转向系统
power steering system 动力转向系统
hydraulic power steering system 液压动力转向系统
electric power steering (EPS) 电动动力转向系统
electric hydraulic power steering system (EHPS) 电动液压动力转向系统
service brake system 行车制动系统
parking brake system 驻车制动系统

Passage Two Power Train

The power train carries power from the engine crankshaft to the car wheels, so the wheels rotate and the car moves. There are two methods in which the drive lines can be designed: the rear-wheel drive lines system and the front-wheel drive lines system.

Task Three 译文

In the rear-wheel drive lines system, the arrangement includes：

(1) The clutch on the vehicles with manual transmissions.

(2) The transmission, either manual or automatic.

(3) The drive shaft, which carries the power from the transmission to the differential.

(4) The final drive, which reduces the speed of rotation, and redirects the line of drive.

(5) The differential, which sends the power to the two rear wheels through the wheel axles.

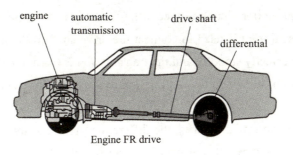

汽车维修初级
（底盘之传动系）

Engine FR drive

The clutch in an automotive vehicle provides a means of connecting or disconnecting the engine from the transmission, both starting up and during shifts.

The transmission provides a means of varying the relationship between the speed of the engine and the speed of the wheels. The manual transmission requires the use of a clutch to remove the engine torque to the transmission input shaft.

In an automatic transmission, gear ratios are changed automatically. This eliminates the need for the driver to operate the clutch and manually "shift gears." The typical automatic transmission consists of a fluid torque converter, a planetary-gear system, and a hydraulic control system. In addition to the forward-gear ratios, neutral, and reverse, the automatic transmission has a "park" position. This locks the transmission to prevent the car from moving or rolling away while parked.

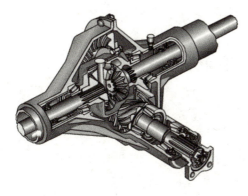

Differential (1)

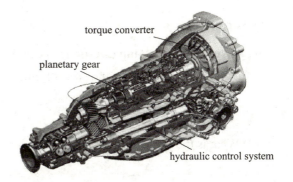

Automatic transmission

Shift lever

Hydraulic control system (valve plate)

The drive shaft (propeller shaft) connects the transmission output shaft to the differential pinion shaft. The universal joint is used to connect the drive shaft to the transmission output shaft. Since all roads are not perfectly smooth, and the transmission is fixed, the drive shaft has to be flexible to absorb the shocks of bumps in the road. U-joints allow the drive shaft to flex when the drive angle changes.

When the car begins to round a curve, the differential pinion gears rotate on the pinion shaft. This permits the outer wheel to turn faster than the inner wheel.

Differential (2)

Differential (3)

Exercises

1. Answer the following questions according to the passage.

(1) What is the function of the power train?

(2) What is the purpose of the universal joint?

2. Make the best answers to the following sentences.

(1) The _____ allows you to connect or disconnect the engine and the transmission both starting up and during shifts.

    A. clutch   B. flywheel   C. brake shoe   D. cab

(2) The _____ provides a means of varying the relationship between the speed of the engine and the speed of the wheels.

    A. clutch   B. drive shaft   C. tire   D. transmission

Vocabulary

Useful Words

clutch [klʌtʃ] *n.* 离合器

differential [ˌdifə'renʃəl] *n.* 差速器

torque [tɔːk] *n.* 扭矩

shift [ʃift] *n.* 换挡

neutral ['njuːtrəl] *n.* 空挡

reverse [ri'vəːs] *n.* 倒挡

flexible ['fleksəbl] *adj.* 弹性的，易弯曲的

bump [bʌmp] *n.* 颠簸，隆起

Phrases and Expressions

manual transmission 手动变速器

automatic transmission 自动变速器

drive shaft 传动轴

wheel axle 半轴，轮轴

final drive 主减速器

gear ratio 传动比

fluid torque converter 液力变矩器

planetary-gear system 行星齿轮系统

hydraulic control system 液压控制系统

propeller shaft 传动轴

universal joint 万向节

U-joint 万向节

Passage Three Power Steering System

Power steering is a system for reducing the steering effort on cars by using an external power source to assist in turning the wheels. Power steering was invented in the 1920s by Francis W. Davis and George Jessup in Waltham, Massachusetts. Chrysler Corporation introduced the first commercially available power steering system on the 1951 Chrysler Imperial. Most new vehicles now have power steerings, although in the 1970s and 1980s it was the exception rather than the rule, at least on European cars. The trend to front wheel drive, greater vehicle mass and wider tires means that modern vehicles would be extremely difficult to manoeuvre at low speeds (e.g. when parking) without assistance. Some automobiles are equipped with a hydraulic power steering system intended to decrease the efforts spent by the driver to turn the wheels and to damp the road jolts

Task Three 译文

transmitted to the steering wheel.

Power steering system

Exercises

Translate the following sentences into Chinese.

(1) Power steering is a system for reducing the steering effort on cars by using an external power source to assist in turning the wheels.

(2) The trend to front wheel drive, greater vehicle mass and wider tires means that modern vehicles would be extremely difficult to manoeuvre at low speeds (e.g. when parking) without assistance.

Vocabulary

Useful Words

commercially [kə'mɜːʃəli] *adv.* 商业上
exception [ik'sepʃən] *n.* 例外，异议
manoeuvre [mə'nuːvə] *v.* 操纵
trend [trend] *n.* 趋势
transmit [trænz'mit] *v.* 传输
damp [dæmp] *v.* 阻尼，抑制
jolt [dʒəult] *n.* 颠簸，摇晃

Phrases and Expressions

rather than 而不是，宁可……也不愿

Proper Nouns

Chrysler Corporation 克莱斯勒汽车公司

Massachusetts 马萨诸塞州

Chrysler Imperial 克莱斯勒帝国

Passage Four   Automobile Transmission

A: May I ask you some questions about automobile transmissions?

B: Sure. Go ahead, please.

Automatic transmission

mercedes-benz-details

Task Three 译文

A: What is the automobile transmission?

B: The transmission is a speed and power changing device. That is, the transmission is used to change the ratio between engine rpm and drive wheel rpm.

A: Is it possible for a vehicle without transmission to move forward?

B: Yes, it is. Any vehicle without a transmission could be made to move but not smoothly.

A: Why can't it move smoothly?

B: Because the vehicle could not get enough power to start. What's more, if a vehicle had no transmission, its start would be slow, noisy and uncomfortable.

A: Oh, I understand. So, in order for a vehicle to get enough power for its smooth start, a power ratio must be provided to multiply the torque of the engine.

B: That's right.

A: Do you know how an automobile reverses its direction?

B: Yes. To my knowledge, the transmission usually provides a reverse gear, which permits an automobile to reverse its direction. Moreover, a common transmission has gear arrangement of neutral position, reverse gear, first gear, second gear, third gear, etc.

A: Oh, you are great! Thank you for telling me so much about the transmission.

B: My pleasure.

Exercises

1. Translate the following expressions into Chinese.

(1) engine rpm

(2) transmission

(3) neutral

(4) reverse gear

(5) first gear

(6) second gear

(7) third gear

(8) torque

2. Translate the following sentences into Chinese.

(1) The transmission is a speed and power changing device. That is, the transmission is used to change the ratio between engine rpm and drive wheel rpm.

(2) To my knowledge, the transmission usually provides a reverse gear, which permits an automobile to reverse its direction.

Vocabulary

Phrases and Expressions

rpm (＝revolution per minute) 转/分
engine rpm 发动机转速
reverse gear 倒挡
first gear 一挡
second gear 二挡
third gear 三挡

Part IV Maintenance and Repair

Auto 4S Shop

The 4S shop auto market model is the product of fierce competition. As the market matures, users of consumer psychology are gradually mature, the diversification of user needs, on products, services, requirements, getting higher and higher, more strictly, and the original sales agent system cannot meet the market demand with the user.

Task Three 译文

Auto 4S shop (1)

The auto 4S shop means the four functions into one vehicle service company, including vehicle sales (Sale), after-sales service (Service), spare parts (Sparepart) and information feedback (Survey).

In general, 4S store brands adopt a regional distribution in one or several stores relatively equidistant, in accordance with the manufacturer of the uniform construction of the design requirements both inside and outside the shop, a huge investment, often millions or even tens of millions, luxury style.

Auto 4S shop (2)

Exercises

Translate the following passage into Chinese.

The auto 4s shop means the four functions into one vehicle service company, including vehicle sales (Sale), after-sales service (Service), spare parts (Sparepart) and information feedback (Survey).

Vocabulary

Useful Words

fierce [fiəs] *adj.* 激烈的

psychology [sai'kɔlədʒi] *n.* 心理学

mature [mə'tjuə] *v.* 成熟 *adj.* 成熟的

diversification [dai͵vəːsifi'keiʃən] *n.* 多样化，多元化

feedback ['fiːdbæk] *n.* 反馈

survey ['səːvei] *n.* 信息反馈

regional ['riːdʒənəl] *adj.* 地区的，局部的

distribution [͵distri'bjuːʃən] *n.* 分布，分配

equidistant [͵iːkwi'distənt] *adj.* 等距离的

uniform ['juːnifɔːm] *adj.* 统一的

Phrases and Expressions

in accordance with 依照，根据，与……一致

Part V Outward Bound

Task Three 译文

Read the following passage and do the exercises.

Electric Power Train

The electric power train for the electric car includes：

(1) The electric driving system, which is composed of different kinds of electric motors and corresponding power electronics, the simplified transmission, and driveline.

(2) The energy storage unit, which typically means lots of battery cells or super capacitors, and a corresponding energy management system. For fuel cell cars, the energy storage unit is the combination of the ordinary battery cell and the fuel cell stack, which converts the chemical energy of hydrogen to electricity.

(3) The electronic control unit, such as the central vehicular control unit for power train and its communication with the on-board E&E (electric and electronic) unit. Sometimes, parts of the control unit or functionality used by auxiliary systems such as the electric air conditioner, electric hydraulic power steering system, and electric brake booster are integrated into the electronic control unit.

Electric power train

Exercises

1. Translate the following expressions into Chinese.

(1) energy storage unit

(2) electronic control unit

(3) fuel cell stack

(4) electric driving system

(5) energy management system

2. Answer the following questions according to the passage.

(1) What is the electric power train composed of?

(2) For fuel cell cars, what is the energy storage unit?

3. Fill in the following table according to the passage.

Electric power train	Composition
1.	Different kinds of electric motors and _____
2. The energy storage unit	_____ or super capacitors, and _____ _____

3.	_____ parts of _____

Vocabulary

Useful Words

corresponding [ˌkɔːriˈspɔndiŋ] *adv.* 相当地，相应地
simplify [ˈsimplifai] *v.* 简化
capacitor [kəˈpæsitə] *n.* 电容器
vehicular [viːˈhikjulə] *adj.* 车辆的，车载的
functionality [ˌfʌŋkʃəˈnæliti] *n.* 功能
auxiliary [ɔːgˈziljəri] *adj.* 辅助的，附属的
hydraulic [haiˈdrɔːlik] *adj.* 液压的，液力的
booster [ˈbuːstə] *n.* 助力器

Phrases and Expressions

be composed of 由……组成
electric brake booster 电动助力刹车
be integrated into 使成为一体，使合并

Proper Nouns

E&E (= electric and electronic) 电力电子

Driving a Car with a CVT

Task Three 译文

A continuously variable transmission (CVT) is a type of automatic transmission that provides more useable power, better fuel economy and a smoother driving experience than a traditional automatic.

The controls for a CVT are the same as an automatic one. That is no clutch pedal and a P-R-N-D-L-style shift pattern. But while an automatic transmission has a set number of gear ratios, usually 4, 5 or 6, the CVT can constantly change the relationship of engine speed and car speed. When driving a car with a CVT, you never hear or feel the transmission shift—it simply raises and lowers the engine speed as needed, calling up higher engine speeds (or rpms) for better acceleration and lower rpms for better fuel economy while cruising.

When you step on the accelerator, the engine races as it would with a slipping clutch or a failing automatic transmission. This is normal—the CVT is adjusting the engine speed to provide optimal power for acceleration.

Exercises

Work with your partner and talk about the differences between the manual transmission, traditional automatic one and CVT.

Vocabulary

Proper Nouns

CVT(= continuously variable transmission) 无级变速器

Task Four

Automobile Body

 **Task Description**

(1) Body construction;
(2) Instrument panel.

 **Objectives**

(1) To understand the main parts of the auto body;
(2) To learn the different body constructions;
(3) To learn how to repair body minor cuts.

Part I   Warming Up

Know About the Automobile Body

1. Work with your partner and answer the following questions.

(1) What is the function of the automobile body?

(2) Can you name any other parts of the automobile body?

(a)   (b)

Automobile body

2. Look at the following pictures, and tell about their Chinese names.

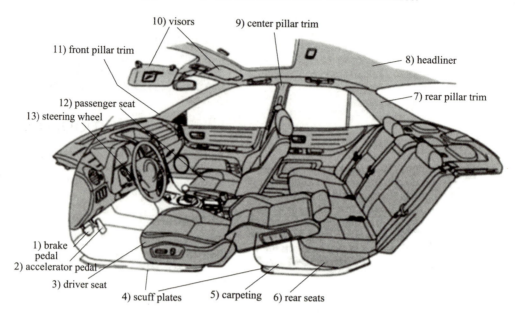

Automobile body components

1)_____ 2)_____ 3)_____ 4)_____
5)_____ 6)_____ 7)_____ 8)_____
9)_____ 10)_____ 11)_____ 12)_____
13)_____

Vocabulary

Useful Words

scuff [skʌf] *v.* 磨损，践踏，摩擦

headliner ['hedˌlainə] *n.* 车厢顶篷内衬

visor ['vaizə] *n.* 遮阳板

pillar ['pilə] *n.* 支柱

rear [riə] *adj.* 后边的

accelerator [ək'seləreitə] *n.* 油门，加速器

pedal ['pedl] *n.* 踏板

dashboard ['dæʃbɔ:d] *n.* 仪表板

Part Ⅱ Listening and Speaking

Dialogue Talking About the Crash Sensor

A: Excuse me, Professor. Can you tell me some information about the crash sensor?

B: Definitely.

A: What is the crash sensor? And where is it located?

Task Four 译文

B: The crash sensor is one of the three basic parts in the airbag system. It is the device that tells the bag to inflate. They are located either in the front of the vehicle or in the passenger compartment, and play a crucial role in driving.

A: What functions do they perform?

B: They can be activated by the forces generated in significant frontal or near-frontal crashes. In this way, the airbag is inflated and protects your head, neck, and chest from slamming against the dashboard, steering wheel or windshield, and significantly reduces the risk of serious or fatal injury in crashes.

史上最强汽车碰撞实验《朗逸VS轩逸》

A: Well, I know. Thank you very much for your valuable explanation.

B: My pleasure.

Vocabulary

Useful Words

airbag ['eəbæg] *n.* 安全气囊

crucial ['kru:ʃəl] *adj.* 有决定性的，重大的

significant [sig'nifikənt] *adj.* 重要的，有意义的

slam [slæm] *v.* 猛击

windshield ['windʃi:ld] *n.* 挡风玻璃

fatal ['feitl] *adj.* 致命的，重大的

汽车碰撞测试 Ford 福特 Galaxy 11

Phrases and Expressions

crash sensor 碰撞传感器

passenger compartment 乘客舱

Part Ⅲ Reading

Read the following passages and do the exercises.

Passage One Auto Body Construction

The body and frame section of the automobile is the basic foundation of

Task Four 译文

the vehicle. All other components and systems are attached to the body and frame.

There are three basic types of vehicle constructions: the body-over-frame, monocoque ['mɔnəkɔk] and space frame. The body-over-frame structure is commonly used in trucks and off-road vehicles. The monocoque structure is used in cars. The space frame structure is used in race cars and buses.

非承载式车身

承载式车身

The body-over-frame car has the separate body and chassis. All the power train components including the engine are found in the chassis and the body is fastened over it. In the conventional body-over-frame construction, the frame is the vehicle's foundation. The body and all major parts of a vehicle are attached to the frame. The frame must provide the support and strength needed by the assemblies and parts attached to it. The frame must also be strong enough to keep the other parts of the car in alignment should a collision occur. To the body technician, the frame is the most important part of the vehicle.

The monocoque body construction employs the same principles of design that have been used for years in the aircraft industry. The main aim is to strengthen without unnecessary weight and the construction does not employ a conventional separate chassis frame. The first automotive application of the monocoque technique was 1923's Lancia Lambda. Citroen built the first mass-produced monocoque vehicle in 1934. In the post-war period the technique became more widely used. The Ford Consul introduced an evolution called unit body or unibody. In this system, separate body panels are still used but are bolted to a monocoque body-shell. The spot-welded unibody construction is now the dominant technique in automobiles, though some vehicles (particularly trucks) still use the older body-over-frame technique. A unibody car does not use a separate frame, but it has a subframe that supports the engine, power train or front suspension. The parts that construct the body in white include the body cover panel and body structure components. The body in white is composed of the side panel, body floor and body roof components.

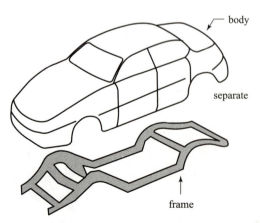

The body-over-frame

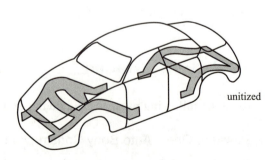

The monocoque

In the space-frame construction, the suspension, engine, and body panels are attached to a skeletal space frame, and the body panels have little or no structural function.

白车身总成补焊工位

宝马汽车底盘车身制造焊接

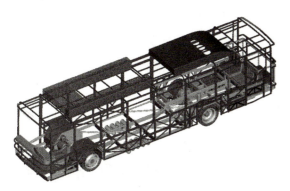

The space frame

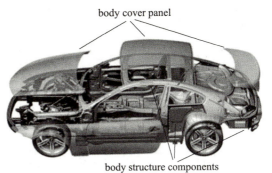

Body components

The body in white

Body structure components

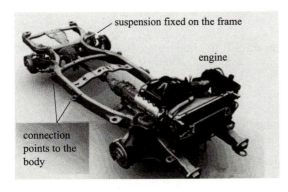

The frame

Body in white assembling and welding

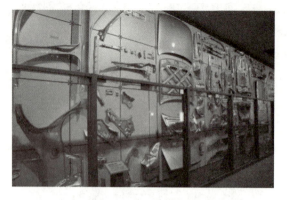
Body in white components

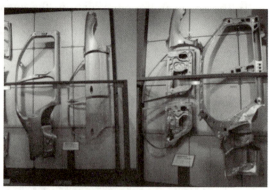
Side panel components

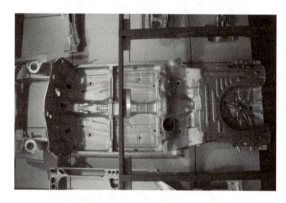
Body floor components

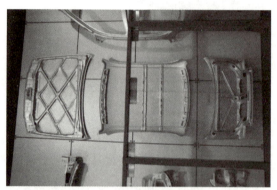
Body roof components

Exercises

1. Translate the following sentences into Chinese.

(1) A unibody car does not use a separate frame, but it has a subframe that supports the engine, power train or front suspension.

(2) There are three basic types of vehicle constructions: the body-over-frame, monocoque and space frame.

(3) The body-over-frame structure is commonly used in trucks and off-road vehicles. The monocoque structure is used in cars. The space frame structure is used in race cars and buses.

2. Fill in the blanks below, and translate the following sentences into Chinese.

(1) The _____ is a load-carrying beam structure of the vehicle.

(2) In the body-over-frame construction, the _____ supports the car body, engine, power train and wheels, and the drive lines and running gear.

(3) In the _____ construction, the frame is the vehicle's foundation. The body and all major parts of a vehicle are attached to it.

(4) In the _____ construction, the suspension, engine, and body panels are attached to a skeletal space frame.

(5) _____ construction employs the same principles of design that have been used for years in the aircraft industry.

Vocabulary

Useful Words

construction [kən'strʌkʃən] *n.* 结构

monocoque ['mɔnəkɔk] *n.* 承载式车身，硬壳式车身

fasten ['fɑːsən] *v.* 使固定

foundation [faun'deiʃən] *n.* 基础

assembly [ə'sembli] *n.* 总成，装配

alignment [ə'lainmənt] *n.* 排成直线，校直

evolution [ˌiːvə'luːʃən] *n.* 发展，演变

unibody [ˌjuːni'bɔdi] *n.* 一体式车身结构

bolt [bəult] *v.* 用螺栓连接

dominant ['dɔminənt] *adj.* 有统治权的，主流的

skeletal ['skelitəl] *adj.* 骨骼的

Phrases and Expressions

body-over-frame 非承载式车身

space frame 半承载式车身

off-road vehicle 越野车

race car 赛车

body in white 白车身

body cover panel 车身覆盖件

body structure component 车身结构件

spot-weld 点焊

Passage Two　Instrument Panel

车上这 10 个信号灯亮，一定要停车

Task Four 译文

Instrument panel

The instrument panel has many indicators and gauges to give you important information about your vehicle. There are five main gauges, namely the temperature gauge, fuel gauge, speedometer, tachometer and odometer.

1. Temperature Gauge

It shows the temperature of the coolant of the engine. During normal operation, the pointer should rise from C (Cold) to Normal band. When you are driving in heavy traffic or uphill in hot weather, the pointer may reach the top of the Normal band. If it reaches the H (Hot) band, the engine is over heating and may cause engine damage. Stop and check.

2. Fuel Gauge

It shows how much fuel you have in the fuel tank. For fuel gauge's proper operation, the ignition switch must be in the OFF position before you add fuel to the fuel tank. It is accurate when the car is on level ground. It may vary slightly while the vehicle is in motion.

3. Speedometer

It shows your speed in kilometers per hour (km/h). On some types, when the speed is over approximately 120 km/h, a buzzer sounds.

4. Tachometer

It shows the engine speed in revolutions per minute (rpm). To protect the engine from damage, never drive with the tachometer needle in the red zone.

5. Odometer

This meter shows the total number of kilometers your car has been driven. The trip odometer shows the number of kilometers or miles driven since you last reset it. To reset it, press reset button to return the trip odometer to zero.

Exercises

Match the English phrases from the passage with their Chinese meanings.

(　　) (1) instrument panel　　　　a. 车速表

(　　) (2) temperature gauge　　　b. 仪表板

(　　) (3) fuel tank　　　　　　　c. 里程表

(　　) (4) rpm　　　　　　　　　　d. 过热

(　　) (5) odometer　　　　　　　e. 油箱

(　　) (6) speedometer　　　　　　f. 温度表

(　　) (7) tachometer　　　　　　g. 转速表

(　　) (8) over heating　　　　　h. 转 / 分

Vocabulary

Useful Words

indicator ['indikeitə] *n.* 指示器，仪器

speedometer [spi'dɔmitə] *n.* 车速表

tachometer [tæ'kɔmitə] *n.* 转速表

odometer [əu'dɔmitə] *n.* 里程表

buzzer ['bʌzə] *n.* 蜂鸣器

Phrases and Expressions

instrument panel 仪表板

temperature gauge 温度表

fuel gauge 油量表

ignition switch 点火开关

Part Ⅳ　Maintenance and Repair

How to Remove Residue Marks Left by Other Objects

This mark on the bumper was made in the underground parking. If you look very closely, it's actually white paint residue over original clearcoat. The clearcoat itself seems to be damaged only slightly. Now, try to remove it.

Task Four 译文

车身划痕和凹陷快速修复

Residue marks

Step 1: Buy ultra-fine 1,500-grit or 2,000-grit waterproof sandpaper (The higher number stands for the finest abrasive: The 60-grit sandpaper is very rough, while the 2,000-grit sandpaper is ultra-fine).

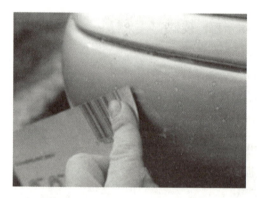

Sanding (waterproof sandpaper)

Step 2: Find polishing compound containing mild abrasives (I used one from Turtle Wax).
Step 3: Find a car wax (I used Turtle Wax liquid car wax with Carnauba).

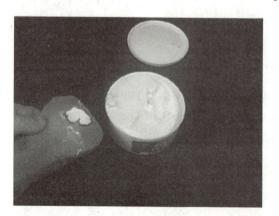

Polishing compound

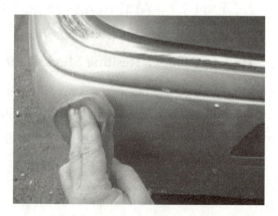

Polishing

Step 4: Try on some tiny spot to see how it works.

Step 5: Sand the marks with wet sandpaper until they all gone (but the clearcoat has lost its shine).

Step 6: Put small amount of the polishing compound onto the damp sponge and rub well until the clearcoat becomes shiny.

Last step: Buff the area with the car wax.

After waxing

Vocabulary

Useful Words

residue ['rezidjuː] *n.* 残留物

clearcoat ['kliəkəut] *n.* 清漆，透明漆

bumper ['bʌmpə] *n.* 保险杠

grit [grit] *n.* 粗砂，砂粒

fine [fain] *adj.* 细小的，精细的

waterproof ['wɔːtəpruːf] *adj.* 防水的

sandpaper ['sænd‚peipə] *n.* 砂纸

abrasive [ə'breisiv] *n.* 研磨料

mild [maild] *adj.* 轻微的，温和的

damp [dæmp] *adj.* 潮湿的

sponge [spʌndʒ] *n.* 海绵

rub [rʌb] *v.* 擦

buff [bʌf] *v.* 擦亮，抛光

Phrases and Expressions

residue mark 残留印迹，擦痕

stand for 代表

polishing compound 抛光剂

Proper Nouns

Turtle Wax 龟博士车蜡

carnauba 棕榈蜡

Part V Outward Bound

Read the following passage and do the exercises.

Task Four 译文

Reducing Body Weight

汽车减重利器

Automotive manufacturers are continuing to reduce the weight of passenger cars to meet the increasing government regulations on fuel efficiency and CO_2 emissions. The body in white is a vehicle's largest structure, and therefore ideal for weight reduction considerations. However, reducing body weight involves a trade-off with body stiffness, a key characteristic which influences vehicle dynamics, durability, and crash worthiness.

汽车造型

汽车造型手绘跑车

汽车的颜色与汽车行驶安全

Body in white

Aluminum has made significant inroads in replacing ferrous materials in certain applications for the automotive industry, in particular in the engine head and block, suspension and some closure panels.However, it has only captured the body in white in limited production run, upper end of the market vehicles.

Exercises

Make the best answers to the following sentences.

(1) Body lightening does all the things below except _____.

    A. raising fuel efficiency

    B. reducing CO_2 emissions

    C. meeting government regulations

    D. saving materials

(2) Aluminum has been used in limited production run for the _____.

    A. suspension

    B. engine block

    C. body in white

    D. closure panel

(3) The reason the body-in-white is ideal for weight reduction considerations is that _____.

    A. it is the largest structure in a vehicle

    B. it reduces body weight

    C. it is the most important structure in a vehicle

    D. it replaces other materials

(4) Body stiffness is a key characteristic which influences the vehicle performance issues below except _____.

    A. vehicle dynamics

    B. vehicle durability

    C. crash worthiness

    D. vehicle stability

Vocabulary

Useful Words

automotive [ˌɔːtə'məutiv] adj. 汽车的，自动的

regulation [ˌreɡju'leiʃən] n. 规章，法规

consideration [kənˌsidə'reiʃən] n. 考虑，原因

involve [in'vɔlv] v. 包含，涉及

stiffness ['stifnis] *n.* 刚度
dynamics [dai'næmiks] *n.* 动力学
characteristic [ˌkærəktə'ristik] *n.* 特性，特征
influence ['influəns] *v.* 影响
durability [ˌdjuərə'biləti] *n.* 耐久性，耐用度
inroad ['inrəud] *n.* 进展
ferrous ['ferəs] *adj.* 铁的，含铁的
application [ˌæpli'keiʃən] *n.* 应用
capture ['kæptʃə] *v.* 捕获，夺取

Phrases and Expressions

trade-off 平衡，协调
fuel efficiency 燃油经济性，燃油效率
vehicle dynamics 汽车动力学
crash worthiness (汽车) 耐撞性
closure panel 闭合板，覆盖件
production run 生产运行，批量生产，流水线生产
in particular 尤其是

Task Five

Automobile Electrical System

Task Description

(1) Automobile electrical equipment;
(2) Air conditioning system;
(3) Bosch Motronic system;
(4) Electronic brakeforce distribution.

Objectives

(1) To recognize the main equipment of the electrical and electronic system;
(2) To learn the main components and functions of the automobile electrical system;
(3) To learn Bosch Motronic system;
(4) To learn the main components and functions of the air conditioning system;
(5) To learn electronic brakeforce distribution.

Part I Warming Up

Know About Automobile Electrical System

1. Work with your partner and answer the following questions.

(1) Can you name some automobile electrical equipment?

(2) If you are going to buy a car, what kind of information on electrical equipment do you want to get?

(3) Can you explain the purpose and the working principle of the EBD?

(4) What are the TCS, ASR, BA, and VDC?

2. Look at the following pictures, and know about the different parts of the automobile electrical equipment.

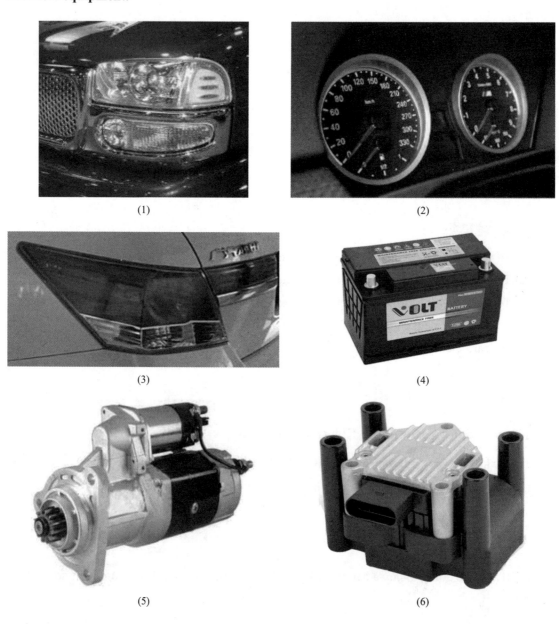

(7)

(8)

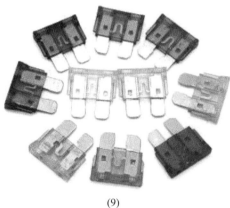
(9)

(10)

(11)

(12)

a. battery
b. headlight
c. taillight
d. ignition module
e. alternator
f. instrumentation

g. air conditioner
h. spark plug
i. fuses
j. air bag
k. instrument panel
l. starter

Vocabulary

Useful Words

battery ['bætəri] *n.* 蓄电池

headlight ['hedlait] *n.* 前大灯

taillight ['teilait] *n.* 尾灯

alternator ['ɔːltəneitə] *n.* 交流发电机

fuse [fjuːz] *n.* 保险丝

starter ['stɑːtə] *n.* 起动机

instrumentation [ˌinstrumen'teiʃən] *n.* 仪器，仪表

Phrases and Expressions

electrical equipment 电气设备

ignition module 点火模块

air conditioner 空调

spark plug 火花塞

3. Look at the pictures of vehicle inspection and maintenance tools & equipment and match them with their English versions.

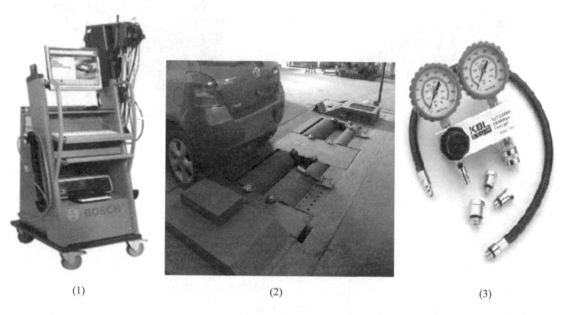

(1)   (2)   (3)

(4)　(5)

(6)　(7)　(8)

(9)　(10)

a. engine analyzer
b. chassis dynamometer
c. cylinder leak tester

d. dynamic wheel balancer
e. engine scope
f. grease gun

g. head light checking equipment h. ignition timing light	i. infrared rays exhaust gas analyzer j. side-slip checking stand

Vocabulary

Phrases and Expressions

engine analyzer 发动机综合分析仪

chassis dynamometer 底盘测功机

cylinder leak tester 气缸漏气率检测仪

dynamic wheel balancer 车轮动平衡机

engine scope 发动机示波器

grease gun 黄油枪

head light checking equipment 前照灯检测仪

ignition timing light 点火正时灯

infrared rays exhaust gas analyzer 红外线废气分析仪

side-slip checking stand 侧滑试验台

Part Ⅱ Listening and Speaking

Dialogue   Automobile Introduction

Task Five 译文

A: Which model are you interested in, Mr. Li?

B: I'm very interested in this model. Would you please explain it?

A: Certainly. I'll explain it from five parts. They are outlook, power and operation, comfort, safety and high price ratio. Now please tell me which part your prime concern is?

B: Safety.

A: Good. The safety of the car includes active safety and passive safety, driving safety and property safety. For example, the ABS belongs to driving safety, and it is a device in active safety. Safety airbags belong to driving safety, too, but they are devices in passive safety. The anti-theft electric lock is a device in property safety. With all those devices, you and your car will be safe when you park and drive it.

B: Excuse me. Could you please tell me more about the ABS?

A: Yes. The ABS is used to control the brakes when a braking wheel goes into a locked condition. Once a braking wheel is locked up, the automobile will slip and have little or no directional stability. In this case, you'll lose control of your car. Clear?

B: Yes. What safety devices is the car equipped with besides these?

A: There are twin front airbags, side airbags, seat belts, EBD, ASR, TCS, ESP, and so on.

B: Sounds great. What is the fuel consumption of the car?

A: It is 7.0 L/100 km(MT) or 7.2 L/100 km(AT).

B: What is the maximum speed?

A: It is 195 km/h(MT) or 180 km/h(AT).

B: Is the car rear-wheel drive, front-wheel drive or four-wheel drive?

A: It is rear-wheel drive.

B: How about the transmission of the car?

A: It has five manual gears and four automatic gears.

B: OK. Let us stop here. Thank you very much.

A: My pleasure. You're welcome to drop in whenever you feel necessary.

Vocabulary

Phrases and Expressions

high price ratio 高性价比
driving safety 行车安全
anti-theft electric lock 防盗电子锁
ABS 防抱死制动系统

Part III Reading

Read the following passages and do the exercises.

Task Five 译文

Passage One Automobile Electrical System

The automobile electrical system includes many parts. An electric motor, called the starting motor, cranks the engine to enable it to draw in a combustible air-fuel mixture for starting. The ignition system furnishes the spark which ignites the compressed mixture. It increases the battery voltage to 20kV which is delivered to each spark plug in turn. The lighting system changes electron flow into light and the horn into sound. If the battery were the only supply of electrons necessary to operate all of the automotive electrical equipment, it would soon become discharged. To prevent this, an alternator, driven by the engine, produces enough electricity to operate the various electrical circuits. The excess is used to recharge the battery. To control the charging rate, according to the needs of the battery, a regulator is connected in the alternator circuit. It causes the charging rate to increase when the battery is low and decrease when the battery becomes fully charged.

Automobile electrical system

To understand the function of your car's electrical system, you should be aware of its major parts.

(1) The battery supplies energy to operate the components when the engine is stationary or when the output from the charging system is low.

(2) The starting system enables the engine to be cranked over at a speed sufficient for it to "fire."

(3) The charging system supplies the electrical energy when the engine is running, and maintains the battery in a fully charged state.

(4) The ignition system provides a spark to "fire" the engine.

(5) The lighting system is needed for exterior and interior illumination.

(6) The auxiliary includes the various accessories such as windscreen wipers and washers, direction indicators, etc.

(7) Electronic devices are used on modern automobiles.

Lighting system

Exercises

1. Translate the following expressions into Chinese.

(1) starting motor

(2) battery

(3) horn

(4) electrical circuit

(5) charging system

(6) accessory

(7) windscreen wiper and washer

(8) electronic device

2. Fill in the blanks below, and translate the following sentences into Chinese.

(1) A _____ cranks the engine to enable it to draw in a combustible air-fuel mixture for starting.

(2) The _____ supplies energy to operate the components when the engine is stationary or when the output from the charging system is low.

(3) The ignition system provides a _____ to "fire" the engine.

3. Choose the best answer to each question according to the passage.

(1) Which of the following will not run if a vehicle does not have an electrical system?

    A. The gasoline engine.

    B. The lighting system.

    C. The safety devices.

    D. All of the above.

(2) Which of the following is a vehicle safety device?

    A. The lighting system.

    B. The starter.

    C. The air bag.

    D. The instrumentation.

(3) Which of the following is not mentioned in the passage?

    A. Electricity provides the spark needed for combustion.

    B. Electricity provides the power needed for starting.

    C. The automobile electrical system provides power for the comfort system.

    D. The automobile electrical system provides power for the lighting system.

Vocabulary

Useful Words

crank [kræŋk] *v.* 摇动，转动

furnish ['fə:niʃ] *v.* 提供

discharged [dis'tʃɑ:dʒd] *adj.* 放电的

regulator ['regjuleitə] *n.* 调节器

stationary ['steiʃənəri] *adj.* 固定的

illumination [iˌlju:mi'neiʃən] *n.* 照明

maintain [mein'tein] *v.* 维修，维护，保持，维持

horn [hɔ:n] *n.* 喇叭

electron [i'lektrɔn] *n.* 电子

auxiliary [ɔ:g'ziljəri] *n.* 附属机构

Phrases and Expressions

starting motor 起动机

electrical circuit 电路

charging system 充电系统

windscreen wiper and washer 刮雨器和洗涤器

electronic device 电子装置

lighting system 灯光照明系统

be aware of 意识到，知道

Passage Two   Motronic Engine-management System

Task Five 译文

Motronic engine-management system, also known as Bosch Motronic system, means combined ignition and fuel injection system in one central control unit. In August 1979, the first automobiles with Bosch Motronic arrived in dealers' showrooms. This date marked the beginning of a new era in engine control. The Motronic system has undergone substantial development since its introduction in 1979.

The heart of the Motronic system is an electronic control unit (ECU) consisting of microprocessor and a memory. The memory contains a work program with data for determining the injection amount and the moment of ignition. The ECU determines which air/fuel ratio the engine runs at based upon engine conditions monitored by input sensors and the program stored in its memory.

Sensors

ECU

    Sensors provide the microprocessor with information on the amount of intake air, engine speed, crankshaft position, the intake air temperature, the engine coolant temperature, and more. The sensors are, basically, the mass air flow sensor, crankshaft position sensor, camshaft position sensor, throttle position sensor, engine coolant temperature sensor, intake air temperature sensor, oxygen sensor, and knock sensor. By comparing the program data, the processor calculates the individual requirements for the next injection and ignition operation. Thus the timing of ignition and the amount injected are quite different in different engine conditions, such as the cases of a cold engine to which strong acceleration is applied and a warm engine subjected to even acceleration.

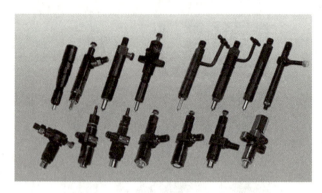

Injectors

Actuators are small power motors that control a variety of engine functions. The actuators are, basically, the injector, ignition module, and fuel pump. Advanced actuators offer increased efficiency, cost savings and environmental benefits compared with mechanical and hydraulic systems.

Exercises

1. Match the English expressions from the passage with their Chinese meanings.

( ) (1) fuel injection system   a. 空气流量计
( ) (2) mass air flow sensor (MAFS)   b. 油泵
( ) (3) ignition module   c. 节气门位置传感器
( ) (4) camshaft position sensor (CMPS) d. 加速
( ) (5) engine coolant temperature sensor (ECTS) e. 氧传感器
( ) (6) throttle position sensor (TPS) f. 进气温度传感器
( ) (7) intake air temperature sensor (IATS) g. 曲轴位置传感器
( ) (8) actuator   h. 燃油喷射系统
( ) (9) crankshaft position sensor (CKPS) i. 爆震传感器
( ) (10) oxygen sensor (OS)   j. 发动机冷却液温度传感器
( ) (11) knock sensor (KS)   k. 执行器
( ) (12) acceleration   l. 凸轮轴位置传感器
( ) (13) fuel pump   m. 发动机工况
( ) (14) engine condition   n. 空燃比
( ) (15) air/fuel ratio   o. 点火模块

2. Choose the best answer to each question according to the passage.

(1) What is the most important part of the Motronic system?

    A. The sensor.

    B. The actuator.

    C. The electronic control unit.

    D. The memory.

(2) Sensors provide different signals for the ECU on engine conditions. Which of the following signals is not mentioned in the passage?

    A. Intake air temperature.
    B. Engine speed.
    C. Oil temperature.
    D. Engine temperature.

(3) Which of the following statements is not true about the Motronic system?

    A. The first automobiles with Bosch Motronic were available in August 1979.
    B. Motronic combined the control of ignition and gasoline injection in one central control unit.
    C. The ECU calculates the optimal injection amount and ignition timing.
    D. Actuators are small power motors controlled by sensors.

Vocabulary

Useful Words

injection [in'dʒekʃən] *n.* 喷射

microprocessor [ˌmaikrəu'prəusesə] *n.* 微处理器

sensor ['sensə] *n.* 传感器

calculate ['kælkjuleit] *v.* 计算

acceleration [əkˌselə'reiʃən] *n.* 加速

actuator ['æktjueitə] *n.* 执行器

Phrases and Expressions

electronic control unit 电子控制单元

ignition module 点火模块

fuel pump 油泵

fuel injection system 燃油喷射系统

mass air flow sensor (MAFS) 空气流量计

camshaft position sensor (CMPS) 凸轮轴位置传感器

engine coolant temperature sensor (ECTS) 发动机冷却液温度传感器

throttle position sensor (TPS) 节气门位置传感器

intake air temperature sensor (IATS) 进气温度传感器

crankshaft position sensor (CKPS) 曲轴位置传感器

oxygen sensor (OS) 氧传感器

knock sensor (KS) 爆震传感器

engine condition 发动机工况

air/fuel ratio 空燃比

汽车空调系统工作原理

Task Five 译文

Passage Three　Air Conditioning System

Vehicles have primarily three different types of air conditioning systems. While each of the three types differs, the concept and the design are very similar to one another. The most common components which make up these automotive systems are the following: the compressor, condenser, evaporator, thermal expansion valve, receiver-drier, etc.

1. Compressor

Commonly referred to as the heart of the system, the compressor is a belt driven pump that is fastened to the engine. It is responsible for compressing refrigerant gas.

The A/C system is spilt into two sides, namely a high pressure side and a low pressure side. Since the compressor is basically a pump, it must have an intake side and a discharge side. The intake side draws in refrigerant gas from the outlet of the evaporator.

Once the refrigerant is drawn into the suction side, it is compressed and sent to the condenser, where it can then transfer the heat that is absorbed from the inside of the vehicle.

2. Condenser

The condenser has much the same appearance as the radiator in the car since the two have very similar functions. The condenser is designed to radiate heat. Its location is usually in front of the radiator, but in some cases, due to aerodynamic improvements to the body of a vehicle, its location may differ. Condensers must have good airflow anytime the system is in operation. On rear wheel drive vehicles, this is usually accomplished by taking advantage of your existing engine's cooling fan. On front wheel drive vehicles, condenser airflow is supplemented with one or more electric cooling fans.

As hot compressed gases are introduced into the top of the condenser, they are cooled off. As the gas cools, it condenses and goes out of the bottom of the condenser as a high-pressure liquid.

3. Evaporator

Located inside the vehicle, the evaporator serves as the heat absorption component. The evaporator provides several functions. Its primary duty is to remove heat from the inside of your vehicle. A secondary benefit is dehumidification. As warmer air travels through the aluminum fins of the cooler evaporator coil, the moisture contained in the air condenses on its surface. Dust and pollen passing through the evaporator stick to its wet surfaces and drain off to the outside at last. On humid days you may have seen this as water dripping from the bottom of your vehicle.

4. Thermal Expansion Valve

Another common refrigerant regulator is the thermal expansion valve. This type of valve can sense both temperature and pressure, and is very efficient at regulating refrigerant flow to the eva porator. Several variations of this valve are commonly found. One of the thermal expansion valves is "H block" type. This type of valve is usually located at the firewall, between the evaporator inlet and outlet tubes.

5. Receiver-drier

The receiver-drier is used on the high side of the systems that use a thermal expansion valve. This type of metering valve requires liquid refrigerant. To ensure that the valve gets liquid refrigerant, a receiver is used. The primary function of the receiver-drier is to separate gas and liquid. The second purpose is to remove moisture and filter out dirt.

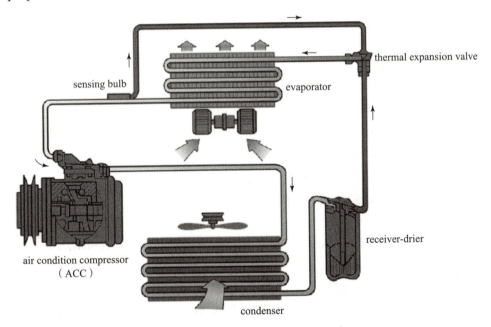

Air conditioning system

Exercises

1. Answer the following questions according to the passage.

(1) How many types do air conditioning systems have? What are they?

(2) What does the evaporator serve as?

(3) What is the function of the receiver-drier?

2. Translate the following paragraph in the passage into Chinese.

Another common refrigerant regulator is the thermal expansion valve. This type of valve can sense both temperature and pressure, and is very efficient at regulating refrigerant flow to the eva porator. Several variations of this valve are commonly found. One of the thermal expansion valves is "H block" type.

Vocabulary

Useful Words

compressor [kəm'presə] *n.* 压气机
condenser [kən'densə] *n.* 冷凝器
evaporator [i'væpəreitə] *n.* 蒸发器
expansion [ik'spænʃ(ə)n; ek-] *n.* 膨胀
refrigerant [ri'fridʒ(ə)r(ə)nt] *n.* 制冷剂
suction ['sʌkʃ(ə)n] *n.* 吸；吸力；抽吸
aerodynamic [ˌeərəudai'næmik] *adj.* 空气动力学的，[航] 航空动力学的
moisture ['mɔistʃə] *n.* 水分；湿度；潮湿
humid ['hjuːmid] *adj.* 潮湿的；湿润的；多湿气的
thermal ['θəːm(ə)l] *adj.* 热的；热量的；保热的

Task Five 译文

Passage Four   Electronic Brakeforce Distribution

Electronic brakeforce distribution (EBD or EBFD), or Electronic brakeforce limitation (EBL) is an automobile brake technology that automatically varies the amount of force applied to each of a vehicle's brakes, based on road conditions, speed, loading, etc. Always coupled with anti-lock braking systems, the EBD can apply more or less braking pressure to each wheel in order to maximize stopping power while maintaining vehicular control. Typically, the front wheel carries the most weight and the EBD distributes less braking pressure to the rear brakes so the rear brakes do not lock up and cause a skid. In some systems, the EBD distributes more braking pressure at the rear brakes during initial brake application before the effects of weight transfer become apparent.

The job of the EBD as a subsystem of the ABS system is to control the effective adhesion utilization by the rear wheels. The pressure of the rear wheels is approximated to the ideal brake force distribution in a partial braking operation. The EBD reduces the strain on the hydraulic brake force proportioning valve in the vehicle. The EBD optimizes the brake design with regard to: the adhesion utilization; driving stability; wear; temperature stress; and pedal force.

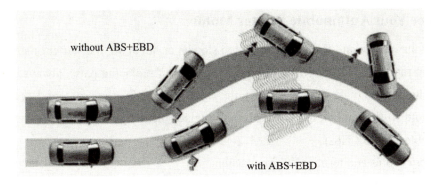

Braking process contrast

试驾全新路虎揽胜运动版

Exercises

1. Answer the following questions according to the passage.

(1) What does EBD stand for?

(2) What is the job of the EBD?

2. Translate the following paragraph in the passage into Chinese.

Typically, the front wheel carries the most weight and the EBD distributes less braking pressure to the rear brakes so the rear brakes do not lock up and cause a skid. In some systems, the EBD distributes more braking pressure at the rear brakes during initial brake application before the effects of weight transfer become apparent.

Vocabulary

Useful Words

technology [tek'nɔlədʒi] *n.* 技术；工艺；术语
maximize ['mæksimaiz] *vt.* 取……最大值；对……极为重视
initial [i'niʃəl] *adj.* 最初的；字首的
application [ˌæpli'keiʃ(ə)n] *n.* 应用；申请
adhesion [əd'hi:ʒ(ə)n] *n.* 黏附；支持；固守
distribution [distri'bju:ʃ(ə)n] *n.* 分布；分配

Part IV Maintenance and Repair

When to Replace Your Automobile Starter Motor

If you try to start your vehicle and the engine turns too slowly, or not at all, the starter or starter solenoid may need to be replaced. Before you go through the steps of replacing parts, always do a few troubleshooting techniques to make sure that the starter or the solenoid is the problem. Because the starter and the solenoid work together, it's always best to replace them together.

Starter Motor Troubleshooting Tips：

(1) Check the battery cables and terminals for corrosion.

(2) Clean the corrosion and replace the battery or cables if needed.

(3) Check the wires to the starter and the solenoid for cracks, corrosion, or breakage.

Make sure your battery is charged enough to perform starting functions. Note: Your instrument lights and dome lights may come on but your battery may still not have enough power to start the car.

检查或更换起动机

Task Five 译文

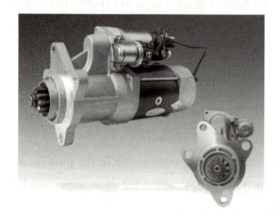

Starter motor

Vocabulary

Useful Words

solenoid ['səulənɔid] *n.* 电磁线圈

troubleshooting ['trʌblˌʃuːtiŋ] *n.* 发现并修理故障，故障诊断与排除

terminal ['təːminəl] *n.* 终端，端子，接线柱

crack [kræk] *n.* 破裂，裂缝

breakage ['breikidʒ] *n.* 破损，断裂

Phrases and Expressions

dome light 圆顶灯

Part V Outward Bound

Read the following passage and do the exercises.

Task Five 译文

Electronic Stability Control

There are two types of automotive safety systems, namely active safety systems and passive safety systems. The conventional auto safety technology is passive, designed to protect occupants during a collision, such as seat belts and air bags. Active safety systems, such as the antilock braking system, blind spot monitoring system, and so on, don't protect occupants in a crash, but help to avoid the crash in the first place.

The Electronic Stability Control (ESC) is an active safety technology that improves a vehicle's dynamic stability by detecting loss and supporting the regain of control of the vehicle.

Skidding

ESC 汽车安全技术演示讲解

During normal driving, the ESC works in the background and continuously monitors steering and vehicle direction. It compares the driver's intended direction (determined through the measured steering wheel angle) to the vehicle's actual direction (determined through the measured lateral acceleration, vehicle rotation (yaw), and individual road wheel speeds).

On slippery roads

电子稳定控制系统的测试

汽车ESC（电子稳定控制）系统以3种方式介入并挽救你的生命

The ESC intervenes only when it detects a probable loss of steering control, i. e. when the vehicle is not going where the driver is steering. This may happen, for example, when skidding during emergency evasive swerves, understeer or oversteer during poorly judged turns on slippery roads, or hydroplaning. The ESC may also intervene in an unwanted way during high-performance driving, because steering input may not always be directly indicative of the intended direction of travel. The ESC estimates the direction of the skid, and then applies the brakes to individual wheels asymmetrically in order to create torque about the vehicle's vertical axis, opposing the skid and bringing the vehicle back in line with the driver's commanded direction. Additionally, the system may reduce engine power or operate the transmission to slow the vehicle down.

Exercises

Match the English expressions from the passage with their Chinese meanings.

( ) (1) active safety system   a. 转向不足
( ) (2) seat belt   b. 横向加速
( ) (3) antilock braking system   c. 被动安全系统
( ) (4) electronic stability control   d. 安全气囊
( ) (5) passive safety system   e. 盲点监测系统
( ) (6) air bag   f. 转向过度
( ) (7) blind spot monitoring system   g. 电子稳定控制系统
( ) (8) lateral acceleration   h. 防抱死制动系统
( ) (9) understeer   i. 主动安全系统
( ) (10) oversteer   j. 安全带

Vocabulary

Useful Words

occupant ['ɔkjupənt] *n.* 乘客
regain [ri'gein] *n.* 恢复，重新获得
intervene [ˌintə'viːn] *n.* 干涉，干预，介入
emergency [i'məːdʒənsi] *adj.* 紧急的
evasive [i'veisiv] *adj.* 逃避的，躲避的
swerve [swəːv] *n.* 转变，转向

understeer [ˌʌndə'stiə] *n.* 转向不足

oversteer [ˌəuvə'stiə] *n.* 转向过度

indicative [in'dikətiv] *adj.* 指示的，象征的

hydroplaning ['haidrəuˌpleiniŋ] *n.* 滑水现象

individual [ˌindi'vidjuəl] *adj.* 个别的，单个的

asymmetrically [əsi'metrikli] *adv.* 不对称地，不平衡地

yaw [jɔː] *n.* 偏航，摆头

Phrases and Expressions

active safety system 主动安全系统

passive safety system 被动安全系统

seat belt 安全带

antilock braking system 防抱死制动系统

electronic stability control 电子稳定控制系统

blind spot monitoring system 盲点监测系统

lateral acceleration 横向加速

dynamic stability 动态稳定性

Maintenance Types

Generally speaking, there are three types of maintenance in use:

Preventive maintenance, where equipment is maintained before break down occurs. This type of maintenance has many different variations and is the subject of various researches to determine the best and most efficient way to maintain equipment. Recent studies have shown that preventive maintenance is effective in preventing age related failures of the equipment. For random failure patterns which amount to 80% of the failure patterns, condition monitoring proves to be effective.

Task Five 译文

Operational maintenance, where equipment is maintained in using.

Corrective maintenance, where equipment is maintained after break down. This maintenance is often most expensive because worn equipment can damage other parts and cause multiple damages.

Exercises

Work with your partner and talk about the differences among the preventive maintenance, operational maintenance and corrective maintenance. Please illustrate them.

Vocabulary

Phrases and Expressions

preventive maintenance 预防性维护
operational maintenance 运行维护
corrective maintenance 修复性维护

Additional Exercises

Match the English expressions from the passage with their Chinese meanings.

( ) (1) automobile body electrical system   a. 电动座椅系统
( ) (2) power window control system   b. 门锁控制系统
( ) (3) power mirror control system   c. 刮雨器和洗涤器系统
( ) (4) power seat system   d. 车身电气系统
( ) (5) power door lock control system   e. 电动车窗控制系统
( ) (6) wiper and washer system   f. 电动后视镜控制系统
( ) (7) ignition switch   g. 点火开关
( ) (8) body control module   h. 电动车窗调节器
( ) (9) local control unit   i. 车身控制模块
( ) (10) power window regulators   j. 局部控制单元

Vocabulary

A

abrasive [ə'breisiv] *n.* 研磨剂，磨料
               adj. 粗糙的
abundant [ə'bʌndənt] *adj.* 丰富的，充裕的
acceleration [əkˌselə'reiʃən] *n.* 加速
accelerator [ək'seləreitə] *n.* 油门，加速器
accessory [ək'sesəri] *n.* 附件
accompany [ə'kʌmpəni] *v.* 伴随，陪伴
account [ə'kaunt] *n.* (关于特定事件的) 描述，叙述
accumulate [ə'kju:mjuleit] *v.* 积聚
acidic [ə'sidik] *adj.* 酸性的
acquire [ə'kwaiə] *v.* 获得，取得
actuator ['æktjueitə] *n.* 执行器
additive ['æditiv] *n.* 添加剂
adhere [əd'hiə] *v.* 坚持，依附，追随
administrative [əd'ministrətiv] *adj.* 管理的，行政的
adopt [ə'dɔpt] *v.* 采取，采纳，采用
agreement [ə'gri:mənt] *n.* 协议；同意
airbag ['eəbæg] *n.* 安全气囊
aircraft ['eəkrɑ:ft] *n.* 飞机，航空器
alignment [ə'lainmənt] *n.* 排成直线，校直
alternative [ɔ:l'tə:nətiv] *adj.* 供选择的；交替的；选择性的
alternator ['ɔ:ltəneitə] *n.* 交流发电机
aluminum [ə'lju:minəm] *n.* 铝
antidote ['æntidəut] *n.* 解药，手段
antifreeze ['æntifri:z] *n.* 防冻剂
apparel [ə'pærəl] *n.* 衣服，服装
appealing [ə'pi:liŋ] *adj.* 吸引人的，极好的
application [ˌæpli'keiʃən] *n.* 应用
approach [ə'prəutʃ] *n.* 方法，处理，对待
apt [æpt] *adj.* 恰当的，恰如其分的
aptitude ['æptitju:d] *n.* 天资，才能
assembly [ə'sembli] *n.* 总成，装配
assess [ə'ses] *v.* 评价，评估
asset ['æset] *n.* 资产，财产

asymmetrically [əsi'metrikli] *adv.* 不对称地，不平衡地
authorization [ˌɔ:θərai'zeiʃən] *n.* 授权，认可，批准
automatically [ˌɔ:tə'mætikəli] *adv.* 自动地
automobile ['ɔ:təməubi:l/ˌɔ:təmə'bi:l] *n.* 汽车
automotive [ˌɔ:təu'məutiv] *adj.* 汽车的，自动的
auxiliary [ɔ:g'ziljəri] *adj.* 辅助的，附属的
　　　　　　　　　　　n. 附属机构
axle ['æksəl] *n.* 车轴，轴

B

backlog ['bæklɔg] *n.* 存货，积压
balance ['bæləns] *n.* 余额
bargain ['bɑ:gin] *v.* 讨价还价
battery ['bætəri] *n.* 蓄电池，电池
bench [bentʃ] *n.* 工作台
biodiesel ['baiɔ:di:zl] *n.* 生物柴油
blade [bleid] *n.* (机器上旋转的)叶片，桨叶；刀片
board [bɔ:d] *n.* 董事会
boat load [bəut ləud] *n.* 许多，大量
body ['bɔdi] *n.* 车身
bolt [bəult] *v.* 用螺栓连接
boost [bu:st] *v.* 促进，增加
booster ['bu:stə] *n.* 助力器
brake [breik] *n.* 制动器；制动
brand [brænd] *n.* 品牌
breakage ['breikidʒ] *n.* 破损，断裂
bucket ['bʌkit] *n.* 水桶
buff [bʌf] *v.* 擦亮，抛光
bump [bʌmp] *n.* 颠簸，隆起
bumper ['bʌmpə] *n.* 保险杠
buzzer ['bʌzə] *n.* 蜂鸣器

C

calculate ['kælkjuleit] *v.* 计算
camshaft ['kæmʃɑ:ft] *n.* 凸轮轴
can [kæn] *n.* 易拉罐
canvas ['kænvəs] *n.* 帆布
capacitor [kə'pæsitə] *n.* 电容器
capture ['kæptʃə] *v.* 捕获，夺取

carbonize ['kɑ:bənaiz] *v.* 碳化

carnauba [kɑ:'naubə] *n.* 巴西棕榈

characteristic [ˌkærəktə'ristik] *n.* 特性，特征

chassis ['ʃæsi] *n.* 底盘

chip [tʃip] *n.* 碎片

chrome [krəum] *n.* 铬

circumference [sə'kʌmfərəns] *n.* 圆周，周长

claim [kleim] *n.* 索赔

clamp [klæmp] *n.* 夹具

classification [ˌklæsifi'keiʃən] *n.* 分类

cleanliness ['kli:nlinis] *n.* 清洁

clearcoat ['kliəkəut] *n.* 清漆，透明漆

client ['klaiənt] *n.* 客户，顾客

clutch [klʌtʃ] *n.* 离合器

coast [kəust] *v.* 滑行

coating ['kəutiŋ] *n.* 涂装

combination [ˌkɔmbi'neiʃən] *n.* 结合，联合

combustion [kəm'bʌstʃən] *n.* 燃烧

commercially [kə'mə:ʃəli] *adv.* 商业上

commitment [kə'mitmənt] *n.* 承诺，保证

commuter [kə'mju:tə] *n.* 通勤者，乘车上班族，月（季）票乘客

compensation [ˌkɔmpen'seiʃən] *n.* 赔偿金，补偿

complaint [kəm'pleint] *n.* 投诉，抱怨

complex ['kɔmpleks] *adj.* 复杂的

compliant [kəm'plaiənt] *adj.* 服从的，应允的

component [kəm'pəunənt] *n.* 部件，元件

compulsory [kəm'pʌlsəri] *adj.* 强制的，义务的

concede [kən'si:d] *v.* 承认，让步

concise [kən'sais] *adj.* 简明的，简洁的

conserve [kən'sə:v] *v.* 保存，节约

consideration [kənˌsidə'reiʃən] *n.* 考虑，原因

constraint [kən'streint] *n.* 约束，抑制

construction [kən'strʌkʃən] *n.* 结构

contaminate [kən'tæmiˌneit] *v.* 污染，弄脏

contract ['kɔntrækt] *n.* 合同

convertible [kən'və:təbl] *adj.* 可变的

　　　　　　　　n. 有活动折篷的汽车

coolant ['ku:lənt] n. 冷却液

corresponding [ˌkɔ:ri'spɔndiŋ] adv. 相当地，相应地

corrode [kə'rəud] v. 腐蚀

corrosion [kə'rəuʒən] n. 腐蚀

cosmetic [kɔz'metik] adj. 修饰的，装饰性的

coupe ['ku:pei] n. 双座小轿车

courteous ['kə:tjəs] adj. 彬彬有礼的

coverage ['kʌvəridʒ] n. 保险，保险范围，保险总额

crack [kræk] n. 破裂，裂缝

crank [kræŋk] v. 摇动，转动

crankshaft ['kræŋkʃɑ:ft] n. 曲轴

crisp [krisp] adj. 干脆的，干净利落的

crucial ['kru:ʃəl] adj. 有决定性的，重大的，关键的，至关重要的

cruise [kru:z] n. 巡航

cue [kju:] n. 提示，暗示，线索

cylinder ['silində] n. 气缸

D

damp [dæmp] adj. 潮湿的
v. 阻尼，抑制

dashboard ['dæʃbɔ:d] n. 仪表板

deal [di:l] n. 买卖，交易

dealer ['di:lə] n. 经销商

dealership ['di:ləʃip] n. 代理商，代理权

debris ['debri:] n. 碎片，垃圾

declare [di'kleə] v. 声明，说明

dedication [ˌdedi'keiʃən] n. 奉献，献身

deductible [di'dʌktəbl] n. 免赔额

define [di'fain] v. 规定；定义

defoamer [di:'fəumə] n. 去沫剂

degreaser [di:'gri:zə] n. 脱脂剂

deliver [di'livə] v. 实现

delivery [di'livəri] n. 交付，递送，交货

deodorize [di:'əudəraiz] v. 除臭味，防臭

department [di'pɑ:tmənt] n. 部门，系，科，局

deposit [di'pɔzit] n. 沉淀物，沉积物

derive [di'raiv] v. 源于

descriptive [di'skriptiv] adj. 描写的，叙述的

designated ['dezɪɡˌneɪtɪd] *adj.* 指定的，特指的
despite [dɪ'spaɪt] *prep.* 尽管，不管
detergent [dɪ'tɜːdʒənt] *n.* 清洁剂
diagnostic [ˌdaɪəɡ'nɒstɪk] *n.* 诊断
diesel ['diːzəl] *n.* 柴油；柴油机
differential [ˌdɪfə'renʃəl] *n.* 差速器
dim [dɪm] *v.* 变暗淡，变昏暗
dime [daɪm] *n.* 一角钱
diminish [dɪ'mɪnɪʃ] *v.* 使变小，使减少
dip [dɪp] *v.* 蘸，浸泡
dipstick ['dɪpstɪk] *n.* 量油尺，测深尺
discharged [dɪs'tʃɑːdʒd] *adj.* 放电的
discolored [dɪs'kʌlərd] *adj.* 变色的，脱色的
discount ['dɪskaʊnt] *n.* 折扣
dispute [dɪ'spjuːt] *n.* 争议，纠纷
dissolve [dɪ'zɒlv] *v.* 解除，解散
distinction [dɪ'stɪŋkʃən] *n.* 区别，差别
distribution [ˌdɪstrɪ'bjuːʃən] *n.* 分布，分配
ditty ['dɪti] *n.* 歌谣，小曲
diversification [daɪˌvɜːsɪfɪ'keɪʃən] *n.* 多样化，多元化
domestically [də'mestɪkəli] *adj.* 国内的；适合国内的
dominant ['dɒmɪnənt] *adj.* 有统治权的，主流的
drain [dreɪn] *n.* 排水管
dressing ['dresɪŋ] *n.* 表面修整，光修
droppings ['drɒpɪŋz] *n.* 鸟兽的粪便
durability [ˌdjʊərə'bɪləti] *n.* 耐久性，耐用度
dynamics [daɪ'næmɪks] *n.* 动力学

E

electron [i'lektrɒn] *n.* 电子
emblem ['embləm] *n.* 象征，标记
emergency [i'mɜːdʒənsi] *adj.* 紧急的
emission [i'mɪʃən] *n.* 排放，排放物，散发物
enclose [ɪn'kləʊz] *v.* 封闭；包装
enforcement [ɪn'fɔːsmənt] *n.* 强制执行
engine ['endʒɪn] *n.* 发动机
engineer [ˌendʒɪ'nɪə] *v.* 设计，建造
enticing [ɪn'taɪsɪŋ] *adj.* 迷人的，引诱的

entity ['entəti] *n.* 实体

equidistant [ˌiːkwi'distənt] *adj.* 等距离的

era ['iərə/'eərə] *n.* 时代，年代

ethanol ['eθəˌnɔl] *n.* 乙醇，酒精

evasive [i'veisiv] *adj.* 逃避的，躲避的

evenly ['iːvənli] *adv.* 均匀地

evolution [ˌiːvə'luːʃən] *n.* 发展，演变

exception [ik'sepʃən] *n.* 例外，异议

exceptionally [ik'sepʃənəli] *adv.* 异常地，独特地

exclusively [ik'skluːsivli] *adv.* 唯一地，专有地

executive [ig'zekjutiv] *adj.* 行政的

exhaust [ig'zɔːst] *v.* 排气，排出

expectation [ˌekspek'teiʃən] *n.* 期望

expediently [ik'spiːdiəntli] *adv.* 方便地，得当地

expense [ik'spens] *n.* 消费，费用

extra ['ekstrə] *n.* 附加条件

extravagant [ik'strævəgənt] *adj.* 浪费的，奢侈的

F

fade [feid/fɑːd] *v.* 褪色，失去光泽，变暗淡

fantastically [fæn'tæstikəli] *adv.* 奇特地，难以置信地

fasten ['fɑːsən] *v.* 使固定

fatal ['feitl] *adj.* 致命的，重大的

fatigue [fə'tiːg] *n.* 疲劳

faulty ['fɔːlti] *adj.* 有错误的，有缺点的

feedback ['fiːdbæk] *n.* 反馈

fender ['fendə] *n.* 翼子板，挡泥板

ferrous ['ferəs] *adj.* 铁的，含铁的

fierce [fiəs] *adj.* 激烈的

file [fail] *n.* 锉刀
　　　　v. 提出，递交

film [film] *n.* 贴膜

fine [fain] *adj.* 细小的，精细的

finish ['finiʃ] *v.* 抛光
　　　　n. 罩面漆，末道漆

firm [fəːm] *n.* 公司

fix [fiks] *v.* 安装，修理

flatten ['flætn] *v.* 击败，摧毁

flexible ['fleksəbl] *adj.* 弹性的，易弯曲的

flush [flʌʃ] *v.* 冲洗，清洗

flywheel ['flaiwi:l] *n.* 飞轮

folio ['fəuliəu] *n.* 页码，对开的纸

forge [fɔ:dʒ] *n.* 锻造，打造

formality [fɔ:'mæliti] *n.* 正式手续，仪式

fossil ['fɔsəl] *adj.* 化石的，陈腐的，守旧的

foster ['fɔstə] *v.* 养育，培养

foundation [faun'deiʃən] *n.* 基础

frame [freim] *n.* 车架

freon ['fri:ɔn] *n.* 氟利昂

functionality [ˌfʌŋkʃə'næliti] *n.* 功能

funeral ['fju:nərəl] *adj.* 丧葬的，出殡的

furnish ['fə:niʃ] *v.* 提供

fuse [fju:z] *n.* 保险丝

G

gap [gæp] *n.* 间隙，空白，缺口

garage ['gærɑ:dʒ] *n.* 车库
v. 把……送入修理厂

gasoline ['gæsəli:n] *n.* 汽油

gauge [geidʒ] *n.* 仪表

generator ['dʒenəreitə] *n.* 发电机，发生器

gesture ['dʒestʃə] *n.* 手势，动作

grade [greid] *n.* 等级，级别

grit [grit] *n.* 粗砂，砂粒

gross [grəus] *adj.* 总共的

guarantee [ˌgærən'ti:] *v.* 担保，保证

H

hail [heil] *n.* 冰雹

hammer ['hæmə] *n.* 锤子

handle ['hændl] *v.* 操作，处理

hanging ['hæŋiŋ] *n.* 悬挂物

hardtop ['hɑ:dtɔp] *n.* 硬顶轿车

hatchback ['hætʃbæk] *n.* 斜背式轿车

haul [hɔ:l] *v.* 拖运

haze [heiz] *v.* 变朦胧，变模糊

headlight ['hedlait] *n.* 前大灯

headliner ['hed,lainə] *n.* 车厢顶篷内衬
headquarters [,hed'kwɔːtəz] *n.* 总部，总公司
headwind ['hed,wind] *n.* 逆风，顶头风
heighten ['haitən] *v.* 提高
hire-purchase ['haiə'pəːtʃəs] *n.* 分期付款购买
historic [hi'stɔrik] *adj.* 历史上著名的
hood [hud] *n.* 发动机罩
horizontally [,hɔri'zɔntli] *adv.* 水平地
horn [hɔːn] *n.* 喇叭
hose [həuz] *n.* 软管
hydraulic [hai'drɔːlik] *adj.* 液压的，液力的
hydrogen ['haidrədʒən] *n.* [化学] 氢
hydroplaning ['haidrəu,pleiniŋ] *n.* 滑水现象

I

identify [ai'dentifai] *v.* 确定，识别
ignite [ig'nait] *v.* 点火，点燃
illumination [i,ljuːmi'neiʃən] *n.* 照明
impart [im'pɑːt] *v.* 给予
impurity [im'pjuərəti] *n.* 杂质
incentive [in'sentiv] *n.* 动机，刺激
indicative [in'dikətiv] *adj.* 指示的，象征的
indicator ['indikeitə] *n.* 指示器，仪器
individual [,indi'vidjuəl] *adj.* 个别的，单个的
inert [i'nəːt] *n.* 惰性的
inexpensively [,inik'spensivli] *adv.* 廉价地，便宜地
inflate [in'fleit] *v.* 膨胀，充气
inflation [in'fleiʃən] *n.* 膨胀，充气
influence ['influəns] *v.* 影响
initial [i'niʃəl] *adj.* 最初的，初期的
injection [in'dʒekʃən] *n.* 喷射
inroad ['inrəud] *n.* 进展
installment [in'stɔːlmənt] *n.* 分期付款
instrumentation [,instrumen'teiʃən] *n.* 仪器，仪表
insulation [,insju'leiʃən] *n.* 绝缘
insurance [in'ʃuərəns] *n.* 保险，保险费
insurant [in'ʃuərənt] *n.* 被保险人；投保人
integrate ['intigreit] *v.* 使一体化，使合并

interaction [ˌintərˈækʃən] n. 交互作用，对话
interest [ˈintrist] n. 利息
interplay [ˈintəplei] n. 相互影响，相互作用
interval [ˈintəvəl] n. 间隔；间歇
intervene [ˌintəˈviːn] n. 干涉，干预，介入
intrigue [inˈtriːg] v. 用诡计取得，激起……的兴趣
inventory [ˈinvəntəri] n. 存货，库存
involve [inˈvɔlv] v. 包含
issue [ˈiʃjuː, ˈisjuː] n. 问题

J

jalopy [dʒəˈlɔpi] n. 破旧汽车（美国俚语）
jamb [dʒæm] n. 门窗侧壁，边框
jingle [ˈdʒiŋgl] n. 押韵，有节奏
jolt [dʒəult] n. 颠簸，摇晃

K

knob [nɔb] n. 把手，球形突出物

L

landmark [ˈlændmɑːk] n. 界标，分界标志
launch [lɔːntʃ, lɑːntʃ] v. 发起，开展，着手进行
layer [ˈleiə] n. 层
lease [liːs] n. 租期，租约
leather [ˈleðə] adj. 皮革的
lender [ˈlendə] n. 贷方
logo [ˈlɔgəu] n. 标识，商标
longevity [lɔnˈdʒevəti] n. 长寿，长命
loyalty [ˈlɔiəlti] n. 忠诚，忠实
lure [ljuə] n. 诱惑，引诱

M

magnesium [mægˈniːziəm] n. 镁
maintain [meinˈtein] v. 维修
maintenance [ˈmeintənəns] n. 维护，保养
manoeuvre [məˈnuːvə] v. 操纵
manufacture [ˌmænjuˈfæktʃə] v. 制造，生产
manufacturer [ˌmænjuˈfæktʃərə] n. 制造商；生产厂商
marginally [ˈmɑːdʒinəli] adv. 少量地，稍稍地
mature [məˈtjuə] v. 成熟
　　　　　　adj. 成熟的

membrane ['membrein] *n.* 膜，薄膜
micrometer [mai'krɔmitə] *n.* 千分尺，测微计
microprocessor [ˌmaikrəu'prəusesə] *n.* 微处理器
mild [maild] *adj.* 轻微的，温和的，轻度的
mileage ['mailidʒ] *n.* 里程
minus ['mainəs] *prep.* 减去
missile ['misəl] *n.* 导弹，投射物
mitt [mit] *n.* 手套
mnemonic [ni:'mɔnik] *adj.* 记忆的，助记忆的
modification [ˌmɔdifi'keiʃən] *n.* 改造，改型，改装
molding ['məuldiŋ] *n.* 装饰条
monocoque ['mɔnəkɔk] *n.* 承载式车身，硬壳式车身
motorist ['məutərist] *n.* 开汽车的人，驾车旅行的人
muffler ['mʌflə] *n.* 消音器

N

negotiable [ni'gəuʃiəbl] *adj.* 可协商的
negotiation [niˌgəuʃi'eiʃən] *n.* 协商，谈判
neon ['ni:ɔn] *n.* 霓虹灯
neutral ['nju:trəl] *n.* 空挡
noticeably ['nəutisəbli] *adv.* 显著地，明显地
nuclear ['nju:kliə, 'nu:-] *adj.* 原子能的，原子核的

O

obstacle ['ɔbstəkl] *n.* 障碍
occupant ['ɔkjupənt] *n.* 乘客
occupation [ˌɔkju'peiʃən] *n.* 职业，职位，占用
odds [ɔdz] *n.* 可能性，概率
odometer [əu'dɔmitə] *n.* 里程表
oil [ɔil] *n.* 油，石油，机油
oppose [ə'pəuz] *v.* 反对；使相对
outlook ['autluk] *n.* 展望，观点
outperform [ˌautpə'fɔ:m] *v.* 胜过，做得比……好
outrageously [aut'reidʒəsli] *adv.* 惊人地
overhaul [ˌəuvə'hɔ:l] *n.* 大修
overheating [ˌəuvər'hi:tiŋ] *n.* 发动机过热
overlook [ˌəuvə'luk] *v.* 忽视，忽略
overnight [ˌəuvə'nait] *adv.* 一夜间，通宵
overspray ['əuvəsprei] *n.* 超范围的喷涂

oversteer [ˌəuvəˈstiə] *n.* 转向过度
ownership [ˈəunəʃip] *n.* 所有权；占有
oxidize [ˈɔksidaiz] *v.* 使氧化，使生锈

P

paint [peint] *n.* 油漆
part [pɑ:t] *n.* 零部件
pedal [ˈpedl] *n.* 踏板
pedestrian [piˈdestriən] *n.* 行人
penetrate [ˈpenitreit] *v.* 渗入
perfection [pəˈfekʃən] *n.* 完美，完善
personality [ˌpə:səˈnæləti] *n.* 品格，个性
petroleum [piˈtrəuliəm/pə-] *n.* 石油
pillar [ˈpilə] *n.* 支柱
piston [ˈpistən] *n.* 活塞
platinum [ˈplætinəm] *n.* 铂，白金
plier [ˈplaiə] *n.* 钳子，尖嘴钳
poetry [ˈpəuitri] *n.* 诗歌
policy [ˈpɔlisi] *n.* 保险单
polish [ˈpɔliʃ] *v.* 抛光
potential [pəuˈtenʃəl] *n.* 潜力，潜能
precaution [priˈkɔ:ʃən] *n.* 预防措施
predecessor [ˈpri:disesə] *n.* 前任，前辈
preference [ˈprefərəns] *n.* 偏爱，喜好
preheat [pri:ˈhi:t] *v.* 预热
premium [ˈpri:miəm] *n.* 保险费
principle [ˈprinsəpl] *n.* 工作原理
priority [praiˈɔrəti] *n.* 优先考虑的事
proactive [ˌprəuˈæktiv] *adj.* 主动的，有前瞻性的
promote [prəˈməut] *v.* 促进；提升；推销；发扬
promptly [ˈprɔmptli] *adv.* 迅速地，立即地
propel [prəuˈpel] *v.* 推进，驱动
propeller [prəˈpelə] *n.* 螺旋桨，推进器
propulsion [prəuˈpʌlʃən] *n.* 推进，推进力
proton [ˈprəutɔn] *n.* 质子
psychology [saiˈkɔlədʒi] *n.* 心理学
pulley [ˈpuli] *n.* 皮带轮，滑轮
pursuit [pəˈsju:t] *n.* 职业，追求

Q

quotation [kwəu'teiʃən] n. 报价，报价单
quote [kwəut] v. 引用，引述

R

radically ['rædikəli] adv. 彻底地，根本地
rag [ræg] n. 抹布，碎布
rank [ræŋk] v. 把……分等级；排列
rear [riə] adj. 后边的
receipt [ri'si:t] n. 收据
recharge [ri:'tʃɑ:dʒ] v. 再充电
recommend [ˌrekə'mend] v. 推荐，介绍
recycle [ˌri:'saikl] v. 回收利用，再利用
reel [ri:l] v. 卷
reference ['refərəns] n. 介绍信，证明书
refinish [ri:'finiʃ] v. 整修表面，再抛光
regain [ri'gein] n. 恢复，重新获得
regional ['ri:dʒənəl] adj. 地区的，局部的
regulation [ˌregju'leiʃən] n. 规章，法规
regulator ['regjuleitə] n. 调节器
rehabilitation ['ri:həˌbili'teiʃən] n. 康复，复原
reimburse [ˌri:im'bə:s] v. 偿还
reinforce [ˌri:in'fɔ:s] v. 加强，加固
relentless [ri'lentlis] adj. 无情的，残酷的
reliable [ri'laiəbl] adj. 可靠的
reminder [ri'maində] n. 提示，提醒
rent [rent] v. 出租，租用
reorganization ['ri:ˌɔ:gənai'zeiʃən] n. 重组，整顿
reorganize [ˌri:'ɔ:gənaiz] v. 重组，改组，整顿
residue ['rezidju:] n. 残留物
restoration [ˌrestə'reiʃən] n. 修复，复原
retractable [ri'træktəbl] adj. 可伸缩的
revenue ['revənju:] n. 收益，收入；税收
reverse [ri'və:s] n. 倒挡
revise [ri'vaiz] v. 修正，校订
revolution [ˌrevə'lju:ʃən] n. 转，圈，旋转，循环
reward [ri'wɔ:d] n. 报酬，报答
rim [rim] n. 轮辋

rinse [rins] *v.* 冲洗掉，漂洗

riot ['raiət] *n.* 暴乱

risk [risk] *n.* 保险类别

rival ['raivəl] *n.* 竞争者，对手

roadster ['rəudstə] *n.* 跑车，双人座敞篷汽车

roof [ru:f] *n.* 车顶

roomy ['ru:mi, 'ru-] *adj.* 宽敞的

rotation [rəu'teiʃən] *n.* 旋转，转动

routine [ru:'ti:n] *adj.* 日常的，例行的

rub [rʌb] *v.* 擦

S

sandpaper ['sænd͵peipə] *n.* 砂纸

scenery ['si:nəri] *n.* 风景，景色，景观

schedule ['ʃədju:əl/'skedʒu:əl] *n.* 计划表；一览表；时间表

scratch [skrætʃ] *n.* 划痕，刮伤，划伤

screwdriver ['skru:͵draivə] *n.* 螺丝刀

scuff [skʌf] *v.* 磨损，践踏，摩擦

　　　　　　　n. 磨损之处

section ['sekʃən] *n.* 部门，地区，章节

sedan [si'dæn] *n.* 轿车

segment ['segmənt] *n.* 部分，分块

self-explanatory [͵self-iks'plænətəri] *adj.* 不言而喻的

sensor ['sensə] *n.* 传感器

sheer [ʃiə] *adv.* 绝对地，完全地

shift [ʃift] *n.* 换挡

sidewall ['saidwɔ:l] *n.* 侧壁，轮胎壁

sign [sain] *v.* 签字，签署

significant [sig'nifikənt] *adj.* 重要的，有意义的

significantly [sig'nifəkəntli] *adv.* 值得注意地，意义重大地

silicone ['silikəun] *n.* 硅酮

simplify ['simplifai] *v.* 简化

skeletal ['skelitəl] *adj.* 骨骼的

slam [slæm] *v.* 猛击

slogan ['sləugən] *n.* 广告语，口号

sloppy ['slɔpi] *adj.* 草率的，粗心的

smear [smiə] *n.* 涂抹

soak [səuk] *v.* 浸泡，湿透

solenoid ['səulənɔid] *n.* 电磁线圈
solicit [sə'lisit] *v.* 征求，请求，恳求
solvent ['sɔlvənt] *adj.* 有溶解能力的
soul [səul] *n.* 灵魂，精神
speedometer [spi'dɔmitə] *n.* 车速表
spin [spin] *v.* 使快速旋转；疾驰
spoiler ['spɔilə] *n.* 扰流板
sponge [spʌndʒ] *n.* 海绵
spray [sprei] *v.* 喷，喷雾
spring [spriŋ] *n.* 弹簧
squeeze [skwi:z] *v.* 挤压
stability [stə'biliti] *n.* 稳定性
staff [stɑ:f, stæf] *n.* 职员，员工
stain [stein] *v.* 玷污
stake [steik] *n.* 股份，股本
starter ['stɑ:tə] *n.* 起动机
stationary ['steiʃənəri] *adj.* 固定的
stereo ['steriəu] *n.* 立体声系统
sterilization [ˌsterəlai'zeiʃən] *n.* 消毒，杀菌
sticker ['stikə] *n.* 标签，贴纸
stiffness ['stifnis] *n.* 刚度
strategy ['strætidʒi] *n.* 策略
streak [stri:k] *n.* 条纹
strip [strip] *v.* 剥去，剥离
stroke [strəuk] *n.* 冲程，行程
struggle ['strʌgl] *v.* 奋斗，努力
strut [strʌt] *n.* 支柱，支撑杆
style [stail] *n.* 样式，风格，类型
substantial [səb'stænʃəl] *adj.* 实质的，大量的
substitute ['sʌbstitju:t] *n.* 代替者，代用品
subtle ['sʌtl] *adj.* 微妙的，敏感的
suds [sʌdz] *n.* 肥皂水，泡沫
sue [sju:/su:] *v.* 起诉，控告
sunroof ['sʌnru:f] *n.* 天窗
supervisor ['sju:pəvaizə] *n.* 监管员
survey ['sə:vei] *n.* 信息反馈
swerve [swə:v] *n.* 转变，转向

symbol ['simbəl] *n.* 象征，符号，标志

T

tachometer [tæ'kɔmitə] *n.* 转速表

taillight ['teilait] *n.* 尾灯

talent ['tælənt] *n.* 天才，才能

terminal ['tə:minəl] *n.* 终端，端子，接线柱

terrain ['terein] *n.* 地形，地带

thoroughly ['θʌrəli] *adv.* 彻底地，完全地

thoughtful ['θɔ:tful] *adj.* 深思的，体贴的

throttle ['θrɔtl] *n.* 节气门，油门

tinting ['tintiŋ] *n.* 着色，染色

tire ['taiə] *n.* 轮胎

tissue ['tisju:] *n.* 纸巾

toothpick ['tu:θpik] *n.* 牙签

torque [tɔ:k] *n.* 扭矩

towing ['təuiŋ] *n.* 牵引，拖曳

transaction [træn'zækʃən] *n.* 交易，事务

transmit [trænz'mit] *v.* 传输

transparent [træn'spærənt] *adj.* 透明的，清澈的

trap [træp] *v.* 诱捕

trend [trend] *n.* 趋势

trick [trik] *n.* 窍门，诡计，花招

trigger ['trigə] *v.* 触发，引发

troop [tru:p] *n.* 军队，士兵

troubleshooting ['trʌblˌʃu:tiŋ] *n.* 发现并修理故障

trunk [trʌŋk] *n.* 行李箱

trustworthy ['trʌstˌwə:ði] *adj.* 可靠的，可依赖的

tune [tju:n] *v.* 调整，调准

twig [twig] *n.* 小树枝

tyre ['taiə] *n.* 轮胎

U

ultimate ['ʌltimət] *adj.* 最终的，极限的，根本的

underlying [ˌʌndə'laiiŋ] *adj.* 潜在的，在下面的，优先的

understeer [ˌʌndə'stiə] *n.* 转向不足

unibody ['ju:ni'bɔdi] *n.* 一体式车身结构

uniform ['ju:nifɔ:m] *adj.* 统一的

upholstery [ʌp'həulstəri] *n.* 装潢，装饰物

V

vague [veig] *adj.* 模糊的，不明确的

van [væn] *n.* 厢式货车

vandalism ['vændəlizəm] *n.* 故意破坏他人财产的行为

vehicle ['vi:ikl] *n.* 汽车，车辆，交通工具

vehicular [vi:'hikjulə] *adj.* 车辆的，车载的

verbal ['və:bəl] *adj.* 口头的，言语的

verify ['verifai] *v.* 核实，检验

vinyl ['vainil] *n.* 乙烯

visor ['vaizə] *n.* 遮阳板

voltmeter ['vəult,mi:tə] *n.* 电压表

W

wage [weidʒ] *n.* 工资，报酬

waterproof ['wɔ:təpru:f] *adj.* 防水的

wax [wæks] *v.* 打蜡

wear [weə] *n.* 磨损

weatherstrip ['weðəstrip] *n.* (门或窗的) 挡风雨条

wheel [wi:l] *n.* 车轮

wheelbase ['wi:lbeis] *n.* 轴距

willingly ['wiliŋli] *adv.* 欣然地，愿意地

windshield ['windʃi:ld] *n.* 挡风玻璃

witty ['witi] *adj.* 诙谐的，有情趣的

Y

yaw [jɔ:] *n.* 偏航，摆头